Moving Forward (Not Moving On)

Praise for *Moving Forward (Not Moving On)*

"In *Moving Forward (Not Moving On)*, Arden Cartrette offers the empathy, validation, and practical support that every grieving parent deserves. This book feels like sitting with a friend who truly understands."

—Lora Shahine, MD, FACOG,
reproductive endocrinologist, Author of *Not Broken*
and Host of the *Brave & Curious podcast*

"*Moving Forward (Not Moving On)* is a sacred offering for anyone navigating the unbearable weight of pregnancy and infant loss. Arden beautifully reminds us that healing doesn't mean forgetting—it means learning to carry our love differently. Through raw honesty and gentle wisdom, she gives language to what so many of us feel but cannot say. We don't move on in grief, we move forward. This book is for the griever who wants to move forward in life after pregnancy and infant loss."

—Erica M. Freeman,
founder and podcast host of *Sisters in Loss*, Author of
Never Healing Alone: For Black Women Silenced by Pregnancy Loss,
When Being Strong Isn't Enough

"Infertility creates a unique isolation—you're surrounded by people yet profoundly alone in your experience. Arden Cartrette has spent years serving this community, and her book does what the best guides do: it sits with you in the hard places without rushing you toward easy answers. She understands that transformation through loss isn't about 'moving on'—it's about finding ways to move forward while honoring what you carry."

—Shara Hutchinson,
Author of *I Still Want to Be a Mom*

"Healing from a loss is one of the biggest struggles for women. This book provides a roadmap to help move forward after a miscarriage."

—Dr. Marc Sklar,
The Fertility Expert, Fertility TV

"This is a must-read for any woman dealing with the trauma of miscarriage. It will leave you educated, empowered, and ready to build the family you deserve."

—Dr. Amy Beckley, PhD,
Founder of Proov

"I wish this book had existed when we were navigating multiple pregnancy losses. It offers the kind of comfort, clarity, and validation I desperately needed—and gives those around us a better understanding of the unseen weight we carried."

—Abby Gray,
Author of *Impatiently Waiting for Miracles*

"Pregnancy loss is an experience that can feel profoundly isolating—but in *Moving Forward (Not Moving On)*, Arden Cartrette offers the compassion, clarity, and companionship so many of us long for. With her deep understanding of grief, healing, and the complexities of pregnancy loss, Arden has created a resource that will be a lifeline for loss parents for years to come. Her words are not just guidance—they are a gentle hug in what is often the darkest moment of many lives."

—Payal Murhammer

"As a postpartum nurse and mother who has walked through recurrent loss and now a pregnancy after loss, I saw myself on every page of this book. Arden's gentle honesty and practical wisdom offer grieving parents the validation and language so many of us wish we'd had sooner. As the chair of a perinatal mental health committee, I am deeply grateful for a resource that is both clinically informed and profoundly compassionate. This book is more than a resource—it's a hand to hold through the silence, stigma, and heartbreak of loss, reminding us that we don't move on, we move forward. I will recommend this book again and again to patients, families, and colleagues."

—Tori Zepp,
postpartum registered nurse; women's health
nurse practitioner student, Duke University

Moving Forward (Not Moving On)

A REALISTIC GUIDE TO GRIEF AFTER PREGNANCY LOSS

ARDEN CARTRETTE

JB JOSSEY-BASS™

A Wiley Brand

Library of Congress Control Number is Available

ISBNs: 9781394324026 (Hardback); 9781394324040 (ePDF); 9781394324033 (ePub)

Cover Design: Wiley
Cover Image: © saemilee/Getty Images
Printed and bound by CPI Group (UK) Ltd, Croydon, CR0 4YY

C9781394324026_060326

*For all of my babies—the two I never got to meet and
my two boys. You give me purpose.*

Contents

Foreword

My name is Amy Beckley and I have survived three years of infertility, two rounds of IVF (in vitro fertilization) and seven miscarriages. Most importantly, I survived all of that to then have two amazing rainbow babies (children born following pregnancy loss). My path was not straight, nor was it easy, but it was damn well worth it!

I have a PhD (Doctor of Philosophy) in Pharmacology which means I have taken so many classes on hormones and how the body works. This led me to believe that it would be easy to get pregnant but, man, was I wrong.

It would take months to get pregnant and then during the first seven weeks of each pregnancy, I would start to bleed and my tests would get lighter and lighter (meaning the HCG hormone was leaving my body). I just couldn't understand why I kept losing my babies and doctors didn't know why it was happening either.

After six losses and two-and-a-half years of trying to conceive, I was given the diagnosis "unexplained infertility." They had no idea why I was losing my babies because all my testing was normal. They told me that the best way to achieve pregnancy was to do IVF, since they couldn't pinpoint the reason for my losses.

My second round of IVF was successful and I welcomed my son into the world. When he was about 18 months old, I turned to my husband and said, "I know I'm crazy, but I want one more."

So we decided to try again. This time I made an appointment with my Reproductive Endocrinologist (fertility specialist) immediately and worked with him on a plan.

As a scientist, I desperately wanted to know what was wrong and why I needed IVF to conceive, but could not conceive naturally. We dissected the IVF process and what my symptoms were to see if we could figure out any clues as to why I was unable to have a successful pregnancy on my own. The thing was, I could get pregnant on my own, I just couldn't stay pregnant. We really discussed the role of those god-awful progesterone shots in the butt (which is where IVF patients are advised to inject them). As my doctor explained, he said that the reason you have to inject yourself with progesterone after a transfer is that progesterone is essential for pregnancy. I immediately thought, "Well, what if I'm just not making enough progesterone, and that's why I keep losing my pregnancies?" What he told me then changed the course of my life forever.

The doctor looked me square in the eye and said, "We just don't understand what enough progesterone is because we don't have a good way to measure it." In all my cycles, I took a 7DPO (7 days past ovulation) blood draw where they would measure the progesterone levels in my blood. Every single time it would show that I had enough progesterone to confirm that I actually did release an egg. But a single level of progesterone from a single blood draw was unable to tell me if my ovaries were producing a healthy amount of progesterone to support the four-day long implantation process. My theory was that I could not have been producing enough progesterone, and that by being given progesterone during IVF, that's what led to my first successful pregnancy. I asked my doctor if there was any harm in just putting me on progesterone after I ovulate naturally instead of going straight to IVF for the second child. He said there wasn't any harm and agreed to prescribe progesterone for my next cycle. Amazingly, after only two months trying to conceive, I got pregnant naturally, but this time I *stayed* pregnant. My progesterone miracle is now 12 years old!

After my son was born, and learning more about progesterone, I also learned that there are many reasons why you could have a miscarriage and there are many reasons why it can be hard to conceive for some people. But I also learned that we don't know enough about women's reproductive systems or their hormones, plus, we don't have enough tools to understand them. And this is what led me to invent Proov.

Proov is an at-home urine-based testing platform that measures hormones across the menstrual cycle to not only tell you when you're fertile, like all the other tests, but also to help you understand how many eggs you have left, and if your hormones are ideal and balanced to support a pregnancy.

There is just so much we don't know about our hormones, our biology, and research is changing every single day. We get new tests, new medications, new procedures that allow those that were infertile yesterday to be able to conceive today. Science is moving at the speed of light. And this is why it's important to educate yourself. As you read this book, this is your first step to having an active conversation with your healthcare provider. You are going to be more successful the more educated you are, and the smarter the questions you ask to your provider.

Arden is one of my dearest friends. Our paths connected when I reached out to her on Instagram in 2017. She was sharing her infertility and loss journey on a blog while also posting on social media about her frustrations with trying to conceive. I recognized that she had a lot of the symptoms that I had such as:

◆ Spotting before your period
◆ PMS-like
◆ Headaches
◆ Short cycles

I knew that I had to reach out to her and see if my experience could help her in her journey.

We became good friends, and I educated her about progesterone, things that she could talk to her doctor about, and ways that she could move her pathway forward and not feel so lost and alone. Arden used Proov to learn more about her menstrual cycle and it helped her see what aspects of her cycle needed more support. It was no surprise to either of us that she needed extra support with progesterone after ovulation.

I think it's safe to say that Arden and I do the work that we do to help prevent other parents from having to deal with the things that we dealt with. Your provider is an expert in medicine, but you are the expert in you. When you come to a provider being more educated on your fertility, that's when you're going to have the most success. This book, the information it gives you, the resources it empowers you with, will help you navigate life after loss in a meaningful and productive way. It's a book that I wish were available when I was trying to conceive and I know that Arden wrote it from the point of view that she wishes she had this information sooner, too.

Wishing you much success in your journey ahead.

—Amy Beckley
Inventor and Founder of Proov

The Purpose of This Book

As someone who has suffered the loss of two pregnancies and had to survive the aftermath of giving birth in the first trimester and managing a type of grief that felt taboo and foreign, I know the importance of picking up a book that feels like it fits with the life experience you're having.

The purpose and goal of this book are to provide you with a sense of having a hand to hold throughout the difficult days ahead and the tools to create a grief plan in navigating difficult events, milestones, and dates that come after pregnancy loss. Whether this is your first miscarriage, second, or more, this book will give you a perspective on "healing" after pregnancy loss that you may not find elsewhere.

My hope is that you'll take what you need from this book—write in the margins, take notes, answer the prompts, and complete the challenges. As you may have noticed from the table of contents, I discuss everything related to pregnancy loss, and going as far as mixing support with education. If you see a chapter that doesn't relate to what you're navigating right now, you can absolutely skip those chapters. But don't forget they are there in case you ever meet someone who needs that support, too.

Introduction

This is the book that I wish you never had to pick up because a miscarriage or any type of pregnancy loss is not something that I would wish on someone. I've always been outspoken and lacked the ability to sugarcoat details or things that are too taboo to discuss, so falling into the role of a miscarriage and bereavement doula came naturally to me. Of course, I wish that it weren't personal experience that brought me this level of passion for reproductive health.

Before being *The Miscarriage Doula,* I held many titles and jobs within the medical field. Helping people on some level was always a goal when fulfilling my responsibility of supporting myself financially. I never thought to become a doula and honestly, blood and gore wasn't something that I was comfortable with. That was, until I had no choice but to get comfortable with it during my first miscarriage. Through *The Miscarriage Doula*, I'm able to provide emotional and mental support to people who are navigating pregnancy loss in real time. It's something that I wish I had during my own losses. Giving people the space to process their miscarriage experience is vital to moving forward, which is why I always aim to validate, educate, and provide insight when I'm working with someone one-on-one.

I've always enjoyed learning and throughout my adult life, I've been passionate about many things, but my passion surrounding pregnancy loss support is one that will never fade or dim because it lives deep in my heart where the memory of my first two pregnancies is held.

My Miscarriage Story

Being a young girl, I loved to read and write from an early age. I found storytelling to be an outlet, and I would sometimes spin stories in my head to cope with the difficult circumstances that surrounded me. I found a way to experience challenging emotions and feelings in the comfort of my own mind. The thought that someone sat down to write the books that impacted me, gave me inspiration as I moved throughout life. To this day, you'll find me with a book (or with my Kindle) in my hands or an audiobook playing through my headphones.

Due to my love of reading and writing, I always dreamed that I would someday write a book that could give its readers the same support and love that other books gave me. However, I never expected that I would write a book about pregnancy loss and the impact that it has on the people who experience it. I guess I never would have expected this to be the book I wrote, because I never thought that miscarriage, or infertility, would happen to me. But don't we all think that at some point?

Unfortunately for me, it did happen, and it changed my life in more ways than I can count on both hands. I often feel these conflicting emotions of gratitude and intense sadness when I think about the fact that I am a bereavement doula. I am more fulfilled than I could ever be, but it cost me years of trauma and isolation as I navigated my own losses. I literally learned from my experiences. I thought, well, how can I learn more about this topic so I can help people cope in real time with this grief?

I'll never forget the moment that a pregnancy test read PREGNANT for the first time. It was then that I felt like I became a mom.

My husband and I had been actively trying to expand our family past the two of us for 16 months. Each cycle that ended with my period starting or a one-lined pregnancy test shattered any hope I had during future cycles.

From the very first month of negative pregnancy tests, I felt desperate for pregnancy and for this life.

Being a mother never felt like a dream of mine nor did it feel like something that I was destined to do. But somehow, in that moment when the pregnancy test confirmed that I was pregnant, none of those feelings I had about my lack of ability to be maternal mattered. That positive test changed something in me, and it felt like a DNA shift, which is the best way I can describe it. In that moment, I became a mom. I became a different, possibly a better, person. It was the first moment that I truly loved someone who I didn't know and cared for them in a way that I never cared for myself. And it was that love that also broke me when this pregnancy ended in a miscarriage because I continued to chase that love far longer than the pregnancy itself lasted.

During the first few days of that pregnancy, I went to the fertility clinic and had blood work done to check hormone levels. I was only met with good news. It felt like things were falling into place. For the first time I wondered, is this what it feels like when something is meant to be? Because I truly thought that this baby was meant to be ours.

Of course, I was aware that miscarriages happen, and I knew the statistic of one in four pregnancies resulting in pregnancy loss but I didn't think—naively—that people experienced both infertility *and* miscarriage. That seemed cruel by any standards. I would check the toilet paper every time I used the bathroom and when I didn't see blood, I kept thinking this is really it!

As we approached the first ultrasound in the seventh week of pregnancy, I noticed that my anxiety was increasing and my ability to push the negative thoughts away was becoming more difficult. This led me to wonder if I had it all wrong. How could this pregnancy be meant to be if I was now worried that they weren't growing in my body? Each emotion felt during those days leading up to the ultrasound felt like a contrast to how I felt during the first few weeks of pregnancy.

At seven weeks pregnant, my husband and I walked into our fertility clinic for an early appointment where we would have an ultrasound and check on the growth of our pregnancy. I knew from Google searches (I don't recommend this) that we should see something that looks like a little bean and a flicker, which means they have a heartbeat. I was prepared to see that on the screen. Instead, I was met with the brief silence from my reproductive endocrinologist and then a "I don't like what I'm seeing here," which followed with tears running down my face. One thing that sticks out from that appointment was seeing my husband's face. He didn't fully comprehend what was happening. It wasn't until our doctor had us sit in his office and we listened to him run through the options that he grasped how terrible this appointment went.

Throughout this book, I discuss different types of miscarriages and how they are treated. In our case, we entered what I refer to as a pregnancy limbo, which essentially means they cannot confirm or deny if there is growth, so they continue to have you come back for ultrasounds. It's absolutely a terrible limbo to be in and we stayed there for three weeks before my physical miscarriage happened. It's a haunting thought to carry around a pregnancy for weeks, knowing they aren't alive, that they aren't growing, and that it's inevitable that you'll have to experience an untimely birth.

My first pregnancy left my body in the early morning of September 26, 2018. I woke to find that I was covered in blood from my pelvic area and below. I switched between the toilet and a hot shower as I felt every contraction. And the oddest element of my experience was that my body lead the way. I pushed with contractions, I knew when I had a moment to breathe. In no way did I physically prepare for a miscarriage, but I experienced my body know exactly what to do in a situation where neither of us was really prepared. Somehow, I both hated my body and respected it at the same time.

Now, my story continues for many months after this miscarriage. With the help of our fertility clinic, we were able to achieve another pregnancy. There was a stark difference in the excitement with my first pregnancy and the gut-wrenching fear I had with the second pregnancy. I was fearful of another loss because I hadn't recovered emotionally or mentally from the trauma of it all.

That pregnancy was different from the start, because my blood work wasn't as good as my first pregnancy, but I didn't hold anything to that seeing as we had perfect numbers and still had a miscarriage. But I had no symptoms, I felt more anxiety than anything else, and I desperately tried to force myself to think positive. I changed the wallpaper on my phone to a photo of a hand-drawn rainbow with the words "think positive" across the top and I took a break from social media so that way I wouldn't see so many stories of loss.

At seven weeks pregnant, we went to our clinic for the first ultrasound. From the moment we walked through the doors, everything felt like déjà vu. Our doctor did the ultrasound and again, there was silence before he said, "This doesn't look good." Because I was looking at the screen, I knew right away. This was going to be our second miscarriage. I went into that miscarriage thinking I've done this before—I can do it again. And then it felt like the joke was on me all along because our second miscarriage was somehow even more traumatic than the first. I felt broken on so many levels.

Looking to the Future

To attempt to end this introduction on a powerful and somewhat happy note—we did continue to persevere. First, we got a second opinion, not because we didn't trust our doctor but because I needed something to give me hope if we moved forward with another cycle at the fertility clinic.

Ultimately, we stayed with our doctor. Our next medicated cycle resulted in our third pregnancy, which gave us our first of two living children.

Every step I took to get to where I am today was difficult. It took a lot of tools, a lot of work, a lot of coping, therapy, and support. This is why I went into bereavement work following the birth of my first living child in 2020.

Throughout this book, I sprinkle in details of my losses and of the clients (names changed to protect their privacy, of course) that I've helped through being The Miscarriage Doula. It was my personal experience with infertility and recurrent pregnancy loss that brought me here and gave me the courage to support others. I use my voice to talk about miscarriage, pregnancy loss, and reproductive health loudly and I provide emotional support to people walking through it—the goal was always to create a space that I desperately needed and couldn't find.

While I'm sorry that you're in need of this book, thank you for picking it up and entrusting me with your grief. Throughout this book, we will navigate life after loss together. I explain and highlight why we never actually move on, but you can move forward instead.

CHAPTER 1

Before Pregnancy

To truly understand pregnancy loss, we must start at the very beginning— pregnancy itself. When I meet with a client for the first time, I invite them to share their story, encouraging them to start at the earliest point that feels significant to them. This could be the moment they first learned they were expecting, or even earlier—tracing back through their fertility journey, past pregnancies, or medical history related to their menstrual cycle. Often, these early details hold key insights into their experience, emotions, and the path that led them to this moment. And it's not uncommon that clients come to me for miscarriage support and admit that while they understood that any type of pregnancy loss was possible, they never expected it to happen to them.

The Foundations of Pregnancy

Pregnancy care often lacks essential guidance, resources, and support, leaving many individuals unprepared when faced with complications or an impending loss. As a result, they enter these experiences with little understanding of what to expect or how to navigate what comes next.

At the time of a positive pregnancy test, women sometimes call their doctor and ask about next steps, often thinking that the next step will be soon, and then they learn that some doctors don't see pregnant patients until at least eight weeks of pregnancy. If you're someone who knows your cycle, is actively trying to conceive, or feeling early pregnancy symptoms, then you could learn about your pregnancy around the fourth week (which is around the time of your missed period). To wait an entire month to see your doctor is where the problem begins with prenatal care. Statistics on pregnancy loss tend to focus on losses that have been clinically acknowledged, meaning there's been blood work done or at least one ultrasound. But pregnancy loss can also happen before someone has the chance to see their physician; therefore, the miscarriage itself may not be clinically acknowledged, leading to a lack of care and fueling the stigmas that come with early pregnancy loss.

Sadly, even if you are a woman who has a uterus and all the moving parts of what's required to achieve and sustain a pregnancy, it can be quite difficult to get to the end of pregnancy and be unburdened by loss.

It's generally understood that roughly one in four pregnancies end in miscarriage during the first trimester. While the risk decreases as pregnancy progresses into the second and third trimesters, it never fully disappears. Second trimester loss and stillbirth are more common than we realize with over 21,000 stillbirths happening every year in the United States. Often, it isn't until someone experiences the death of their child in utero that they truly grasp how fragile life is from the moment of conception.

For me, it was overwhelming to realize just how many obstacles stand in the way of a successful pregnancy—and how miraculous it is that any of us exist at all. At the same time, it made me question: Why did that baby survive when mine didn't? But science isn't a perfect formula and, sadly, life isn't always fair. It's a difficult way to realize those aspects of life and it makes coping all the more difficult because what we once thought we knew and what we now know are two different things. Those who have experienced pregnancy loss understand this on a much deeper level.

To start talking about pregnancy loss in the most cohesive way possible, I first discuss the foundations of pregnancy and the basics of conception, mainly because many people don't know how it all works. And it's not their fault because we truly aren't taught about the phases of our cycles, how important specific hormones are (for avoiding pregnancy and for achieving a healthy, viable one), and the risks involved between conception and the first trimester (because there are a lot).

I know firsthand from my own experiences, as well as from working with thousands of women on the topic, that many women immediately jump to, "I should have done more research" or "Why didn't I know this?" And it's not our fault—if anything, it's the education we are handed and the lack of resources that are shared with us from a young age. The good news is that we can break that cycle and continue to learn from each other, using social media as a tool, buying books, and supporting the women in the world whose mission it is to teach us these things. We can pass that along to others, hopefully our own children, and truly break this cycle of unawareness within our own bodies.

The good news is that by purchasing this book, you are taking a step forward. As we navigate these topics surrounding pregnancy and loss, you might feel hindsight bias pop up and tell you that you should have known this. Let's call it what it is—wishing you knew then what you're about to learn. That's a perfectly normal human response to grief and moving forward.

The Phases of the Menstrual Cycle

Speaking in basic terms, a *menstrual cycle* is a hormonal cycle that is part of the female reproductive system. A cycle may vary in length but essentially includes the growth of a follicle, its release, and either the shedding of uterine lining, or a pregnancy that is achieved with an embryo that implants in the uterine wall.

During one menstrual cycle, you circle through four phases: menstruation, the follicular phase, ovulation, and the luteal phase. Each of these phases has a very important role in menstrual health but also in achieving pregnancy if that's your goal. You may also get an insight into your overall health once you track your cycle efficiently and understand each phase.

If you are someone who has a period tracking app, you may only note what day your cycle began on (when you started bleeding), the duration of the bleeding, and when your cycle ends (or another begins). However, there are factors to pay attention to between the beginning and end of your cycle.

You may be someone who doesn't need to focus on their menstrual cycle, maybe because you are pursuing fertility treatments such as IUI or IVF or because you are in a same-sex relationship and you aren't worried about a pregnancy. No matter what path you're on now, it can be helpful to know more about your cycle. That way, you get a deeper insight into your reproductive health. It can be beneficial even if you are doing treatment and not conceiving at home unassisted. It's not always as cut and dried as it seems from the lackluster information we learned during the sex-ed course in middle school.

MENSES

The first phase, *menstruation*, is also referred to as *menses*. I've had many clients who expressed their loathing of the first phase in their menstrual cycle and it's always for various reasons. Whether it indicates that another month of trying to conceive has passed and they aren't pregnant, it's triggering past pregnancy loss, or they have an unpredictable cycle and it's never something they can prepare for like some others can—there are a lot of reasons not to enjoy the menses phase.

Amy, a client of mine (named changed to protect her privacy), has PCOS (*polycystic ovary syndrome*), which caused her to feel frustrated with her body because she never knows when her period will arrive. Trying to conceive is naturally harder for her because she doesn't always ovulate a healthy follicle due to her polycystic ovaries. She also must wait a lengthy amount of time before knowing if a cycle failed or resulted in a pregnancy. So, for Amy, the menstrual aspect of her cycle is both something she dreads but feels relieved by. I've told her countless times that it's normal to feel relieved—I bet some people reading this book can relate to that feeling as well. For someone with PCOS, getting a period marks the end of a cycle and it's often a time where you can catch your breath after holding it for 40–60 days (sometimes more).

During this phase, you'll have your period and a menstrual bleed. The level of bleeding varies person to person but should never be too light or too heavy. I know this can be frustrating advice, seeing as we never really know exactly what that means. The range of "normal" bleeding during menses is as little as 5 ml and can extend to well over 100 ml. However, every resource or study seems to have a different range. It can be difficult to know if your bleeding is normal because we aren't often measuring our blood as it exits the body. (Although you can use a menstrual disc if you want to get a better idea about how much blood you're losing in a period.)

The main concern during this phase regarding fertility health is whether you have a period that is too light (which could indicate an issue with producing progesterone) or too heavy (which might indicate other issues like ovarian cysts, polyps, etc.). It's important to note how many days you bleed, what your bleeding pattern is like (days of light bleeding versus days of heavy bleeding), and the consistency of the blood, such as the presence of blood clots or the thickness of blood—sometimes people will comment if their blood feels sticky or if it seems to be mixed with mucus.

If you are working with a fertility clinic during this phase, they often do what's referred to as a *baseline ultrasound*, which is a vaginal ultrasound that looks at your uterus, fallopian tubes, and ovaries prior to medications and treatment. Even when you're working with a fertility clinic, the details of your cycle, especially your menstruation patterns, are still important information to understand. It might help them understand if they see that your uterine lining is too thin or very thick, for example.

THE FOLLICULAR PHASE

The second phase is known as the *follicular phase*. Estrogen is the dominant hormone in your reproductive system during this phase because your body is preparing for ovulation. During this stage, your follicles will focus on growth, thanks to estrogen and a hormone referred to as FSH (*follicle-stimulating hormone*), which increases the quality of the follicle and promotes healthy egg quality.

This phase begins after the period and lasts until ovulation happens, which varies from body to body. Since most people tend to ovulate between days 10–25 of their cycle, this phase can be long or short.

During this phase of your cycle, you may use at-home ovulation test strips. They test for a hormone referred to as LH (*luteinizing hormone*), which also helps prepare your body for ovulation. It's the signal to your fallopian tubes that they can release the follicle (or follicles) that you've been growing throughout the last week or two. Inside the follicle will be an egg and that egg is either an oocyte (an immature egg) or an ovum (a mature egg). If that follicle (and egg) is fertilized, meaning the sperm properly embeds, then that follicle would later become an embryo.

When testing for your LH levels at home, you'll notice that these tests will refer to a "peak," which essentially means your LH level is the highest it will be that cycle and that ovulation will occur within the next 48 hours.

If you're working with a fertility clinic, this might be where you take stimulating medications—whether you're doing a medicated cycle and still having sex to achieve pregnancy or doing an IUI (*intrauterine insemination*) or an IVF (*in vitro fertilization*) cycle. You will also have many appointments at the clinic during this phase, as they want to ensure that the medications are working and things are on track for your treatment.

OVULATION

The third phase of a menstrual cycle is *ovulation*. Following a peak ovulation test or if you're charting using other methods, ovulation will occur. This is the time where your follicle is either fertilized or not. Unfortunately, it takes a few days for us to know if fertilization has occurred. This is the main event for a cycle if you're hoping to achieve a pregnancy.

When working with clients, I often say that after this point, it's out of our hands and we've done the work we can do. It's both scary to think of and often freeing, because the first half of the cycle is spent worrying about the timing of ovulation and hoping that you get everything done at the right time.

For those who are doing fertility treatment or working with a fertility specialist, they often are inducing ovulation with medications that stimulate the reproductive system. So instead of relying on at-home ovulation tests, you may follow the direction of your doctor, who then assists in inducing ovulation on time.

THE LUTEAL PHASE
The final phase, and arguably the most important phase in a cycle, is the *luteal phase*. During this phase, progesterone rises (with or without the assistance of prescription medication) and, hopefully, a fertilized follicle (an embryo) will find a nice, homey spot in the uterus where it can grow and thrive.

For many potential pregnancies, this is the first hurdle. There are a lot of developmental milestones for the embryo during this time. The uterus also plays a large role during this stage, and the hormones have to be just right for implantation.

With a spontaneous or natural conception, implantation often occurs 7–10 days after ovulation. Happening earlier doesn't guarantee a positive outcome just like a late implantation won't be a warning sign for an anticipated loss. Following an insemination (through IUI or IVF), implantation of the embryo will occur within or 5–10 days. The reason why the days are different is because with an IVF transfer, the embryo is already created and so the time frame of expected implantation might be less than a spontaneous conception. If a pregnancy has occurred, it can be detected on blood work or with an at-home pregnancy test 10–14 days after ovulation and in IVF cycles, fertility clinics often do a blood test to confirm pregnancy as early as 7 days post-insemination.

Risks Associated with Pregnancy

Pregnancy, at its baseline, is a risk to the body and mind of a pregnant human being. But the apps and the online articles don't like to talk about how fragile life is from conception because it scares the majority of their readers. It's a hard line to walk, because people should be informed and not inundated with everything that could go wrong in a pregnancy.

Following a menstrual cycle—regardless of it being unassisted conception or conception through fertility treatments—you are either pregnant or aren't and there are a lot of mixed emotions that come along with a cycle ending with either outcome.

Let's start by talking about conception that happens without the assistance of IVF and then we will circle back to including IVF into the topic because there are things to discuss from every angle of conception.

WHEN A CYCLE DOESN'T RESULT IN PREGNANCY

When a menstrual cycle doesn't result in a pregnancy, there are a few reasons why. Either fertilization didn't happen *or* a follicle was fertilized (by sperm) but didn't survive the embryo developmental process. It's also possible that the fertilized embryo didn't implant itself on the uterine wall and after 12–14 days (in a healthy cycle), the cycle will end. The next menstrual bleed (menses) will occur, marking the end of one cycle and the beginning of another.

It's important to note that there is no current way to differentiate between these three approaches that all result in no pregnancy. When someone is struggling to get pregnant, they may assume that all the stages aren't happening and that their eggs and partner's sperm (or donor's sperm) aren't a match somehow.

However, it's important to remember that even when a cycle ends without a pregnancy, it doesn't mean that other things aren't happening in the uterus. It's just not all the right steps. Most of the time, this is related to hormones, which highlights the importance of tracking your cycle and looking for signs that could be related to your fertility in general.

From the outside, conception seems simple, right? But it's complex and there are many minuscule steps that must happen.

RISKS ASSOCIATED WITH ART (ASSISTED REPRODUCTIVE TECHNOLOGY) PREGNANCIES

Now let's say that the cycle does result in a positive pregnancy test. The first few weeks of a pregnancy are very fragile, which is why the risk of pregnancy loss is so high. Developmentally, an embryo has attached itself to the uterine wall, the ovaries are working overtime to produce hormones such as progesterone, and the embryo is growing each day, developing everything needed to become a fetus.

Things that can go "wrong" during this stage can be developmental, where the embryo simply does not develop as needed or is missing a key part of development. Blood clots can occur around the reproductive system that can be a threat to the blood flow to the pregnancy, hormonal shifts can go undetected, infections happen, and chromosomal abnormalities can occur. The risks in early pregnancy are high.

An IVF pregnancy is not exempt from risk of miscarriage or complications, even though the assumption is that IVF is some kind of guarantee. While it helps people achieve pregnancy, there is a higher risk of high blood pressure, low birth weight, preeclampsia, and placental concerns. Most people who use assisted reproductive technology (ART) are monitored based on these factors and may even see a high-risk doctor called a Maternal Fetal Medicine (MFM) physician. A pregnancy conceived with the assistance of reproductive technology and care means that the pregnant person often has more medical care earlier in pregnancy, which is helpful. The IVF protocol might include progesterone injections, blood thinners, and sometimes even antibiotics to avoid infections that can cause pregnancy loss. However, as an IVF pregnancy progresses, there's a higher risk of preeclampsia or cervical insufficiencies, as well as something called "retained products of conception," whether that pregnancy ends with a living child or not.

> While you might see many happy pictures of pregnancy on your social media feeds and in movies or TV shows, they are often not discussing the stresses of pregnancy or of getting pregnant. Maybe those people have been lucky enough to not experience them, or maybe they only share the good news on their social media feeds. You probably don't know what, possibly difficult, journey they had to take to get to that point.

ADVOCATING FOR YOURSELF

You may be wondering how you can advocate for yourself early in pregnancy. Well, the bad news is that there's not much you can do to control the outcome of a pregnancy, especially at this early stage. As I mentioned, even pregnancies achieved with the assistance of a fertility specialist can end in pregnancy loss, so we aren't ever safe. This is what I refer to as a "hard truth," because it's something that no one else wants to tell you.

What you can do is look at your pregnancy history and ask yourself, "How would I change my experience?" Use that to fuel how you request your medical team's support.

For example, I asked for earlier and more frequent ultrasounds. Having a missed miscarriage, I never wanted to sit with my dead baby inside my body for weeks ever again.

For you, it might be more blood work to check hormone levels, more ultrasounds, finding a new care team who is compassionate and validating, being more private about pregnancy, being more public, and so on.

The Physical and Emotional Journey of Pregnancy

Before someone even has a miscarriage, the beginning of pregnancy is difficult. Whether it's because the symptoms of pregnancy are weighing them down, they are overwhelmed about the changes that are coming, or they are struggling with anxiety, depression, or feeling unsupported by those around them—there are a lot of challenges that play a huge role in the emotional journey of pregnancy.

Society adds another element of pressure. There's an unspoken rule to wait until 12 weeks to announce a pregnancy on social media, even though you don't even *have* to announce on social media to begin with—that's yet another pressure. Ensuring that you're eating the right things, doing the right things, and so on—it's exhausting to live up to what society paints as the perfect pregnancy.

I remember when my husband and I were trying to conceive. I was determined to have the perfect pregnancy. From the brand of prenatal vitamins, to planning maternity fashion (even though I was a terribly unfashionable person), to thinking about what our home would look like with a baby and planning to have the best of the best. Because that's what I saw online. The societal element played such a huge role that I felt ashamed of telling anyone that we were trying to conceive. I was embarrassed that we had been trying for multiple months, plus I didn't want my employer to find out due to the fear that they would learn that I was a woman who wanted to have children. I felt like I had to keep this huge secret.

Then when I was pregnant, I kept it a secret, too. I wrote on an anonymous blog at the time because I was so lonely in my quest to parenthood that I needed to find some sort of community or connection. On that blog, I didn't show my face or use my first name so it felt like a safe space to share the innermost emotions.

Then I had my miscarriage and everything imploded. I felt like I had no choice but to tell my boss because I had to call out of work and wait three weeks before my physical miscarriage happened. I felt like society did nothing but set me up for loneliness.

I knew by the morning after my loss that I never wanted to feel that ashamed or isolated again, so I took the route of talking very loudly about pregnancy loss. It's that feeling of being fed up with the secrets that led me to write these words and I'm thankful for that. At the same time, I'll never forget what it felt like to want to scream into the void that I had a miscarriage and that I was no longer the person everyone thought they knew. I wish that society could support pregnancy loss better. That would be much better than the loneliness that comes with navigating miscarriage after miscarriage.

Reflection Prompts

- ◆ Prior to your first pregnancy, what do you remember about your expectations or beliefs? Did you feel well educated about your cycle and the risk of loss?
- ◆ Over time, since puberty, how has your relationship with your body changed? How has your experience with trying to conceive and/or pregnancy loss shifted that view?
- ◆ What parts of this chapter made you pause or feel something deeply? Note what resonated with you—whether it was a statistic, a shared emotion, or a new piece of information. What might you want to explore or learn more about?

CHAPTER 2

Understanding Pregnancy Loss

There aren't many feelings that compare to seeing two lines on a pregnancy test, or the words PREGNANT if you're using a digital pregnancy test. Many women feel excitement that's mixed with fear and immediately start wondering what the future will look like with this addition to their family. Of course, some people are surprised by this news, while others have taken all of the necessary steps to achieve a positive pregnancy test. It doesn't matter *how* someone got here, in a circumstance where a pregnancy is desired on any level, the feelings are often very similar.

Pregnancy loss is a unique and deeply personal grief. It is the loss of a life that began within you, one that your body nurtured for as long as it could, only for that life to end while you are left to carry the weight of its absence. The truth is, unless someone has experienced this loss firsthand—or possesses an extraordinary depth of empathy—it is nearly impossible to fully grasp its magnitude.

Losing Your Dream, Your Plans, and a Little of Yourself

In many ways, experiencing a miscarriage or giving birth to a baby who isn't alive is like losing a part of yourself—an amputation that happens in the most devastating way. A removal that leaves nerves exposed and vulnerable while you desperately try to find your way back to who you were before. Being pregnant is like a promotion in life, right? You get this new experience that's sometimes difficult (such as being nauseous, more tired, or hungry) but also beautiful because you know that you're growing a human life. But then the promotion is taken from you and the new title that you would have had is stripped (as far as society is concerned). Returning to your life as it was before is difficult and instead you have to pave a new path. It's a path that you likely don't want to go down. You just want your baby back.

Just because your baby wasn't born, say, doesn't mean you don't experience grief when you lose them. There's more to despair than an outward physical connection that is visible from the outside of your body. Psychologist

John Bowlby, author of *Attachment and Loss*,[1] focused his life's work on understanding attachment theory between children and their caregivers, specifically the primary caregiver. Through his work, he highlighted how deep-rooted the connection is between mother and child, even during pregnancy. If you think of it as an attachment, then the loss feels more like an amputation than losing something.

When I meet with a client for the first time, I often say, it's lovely to meet you, though I wish we were meeting under different circumstances. While I've said it countless times, I mean it each time. There are many unfair things that happen in life. We are in a day and age where we have easy access to the Internet and can research to understand what's happened to us. It's a way for us to seek support and guidance, but so much of what we find feels impersonal. This is why, in my work, I aim to make women feel like they are speaking to a friend even though they are only just meeting me. I know from experience that I needed a friend who would understand, and that was hard to come by.

Life after pregnancy loss is incredibly hard. Seeking support requires vulnerability, and trusting someone with your story is no small act. Many people that I talk to express that they either don't have support in their everyday lives or that their support isn't what they need, which can cause them to feel invalided in their grief.

For a moment, I want to speak to you as I would a client—walking with you through the emotions that surface as you begin to process your loss. It doesn't matter if your loss is unfolding as you read this, if it happened a month ago, a year ago, or many years ago—you deserve the space to feel what's rising in your chest. Grief isn't something we can bypass. There's no fast-forward button; no way to skip over the parts that feel unbearable. But here's the truth: the way through grief is to name it, to acknowledge it, and to find your own way forward—one step at a time.

When it comes to writing a book about pregnancy loss, I immediately knew that I wanted to mix education with validation. From personal experience,

I felt lost because miscarriage was never something I searched the Internet for—until it happened to me. And even then, it was difficult to understand the terms, the diagnoses, or the treatment options. I felt like I needed to get a college degree just to be a patient experiencing infertility and pregnancy loss.

It shouldn't be like that and, unfortunately, for so many—it is exactly like that. Whenever I meet with clients one-on-one, they often have questions about their diagnosis, or they ask if they chose the right option when executing the loss process. Or people feel like they don't have any option and need to cope with that. The bottom line is simply that education and information make us more informed, which not only helps when advocating for ourselves but also helps as we cope with the loss.

My first miscarriage was categorized as a missed miscarriage, but the doctor wasn't sure if it was a blighted ovum because my gestational sac kept growing while the yolk sac (the pregnancy itself) didn't. This led me to wonder if I was ever really pregnant in the first place and that thought process really impacted my grief. And if this paragraph made no sense to you, then it probably shows just how little we understand about pregnancy loss. Don't worry, we are going to discuss this further.

In this chapter, I go through every type of pregnancy loss and explain what it is, what it means, and how it's usually medically treated. The goal is for you to understand your loss better and have the information as a coping tool as you move forward through your grief.

Terminology Related to Pregnancy (and Loss)

At the first ultrasound during my first pregnancy, which is where we learned that we weren't seeing what we needed to—my fertility doctor mentioned a yolk sac, a fetal pole, and the possibility of a blighted ovum. First, I felt shocked and confused that I could possibly be having a miscarriage and then the thoughts of not understanding what these terms meant settled in as well. I cried the entire way home (of course) and through this feeling of shock, I searched the Internet for every unfamiliar word that was said.

Looking back on those moments, I believed that if I could understand the terms better, I could somehow fix this. As if it were fixable in the first place. And then when I had my physical miscarriage, I saw the word *complete abortion* on my medical documents and felt so much anger that I had abortion on my medical documents. Politics aside, the guilt and shame associated with that word were painful to see.

As I've supported thousands of people through pregnancy loss, the topic of terminology comes up often. It's intertwined in our grief in ways that we don't understand until we better understand our losses. It's for this reason that I dedicate pages of this book to discussing the terms that we hear often, in a way that feels informative yet supportive—not as medical as what you'll find on the Internet.

THE ANATOMY OF PREGNANCY

Starting with the anatomy of a pregnancy—inside a uterus there's a *gestational sac,* which can be seen on an ultrasound very early on. The gestational sac both confirms pregnancy in the uterus (especially if a medical provider is worried about an ectopic pregnancy) and is the first layer of protection, a barrier, for the pregnancy itself.

The next layer is the *amniotic sac,* which is the sac of amniotic fluid that surrounds the baby. Between five- and seven-weeks of gestation, you'll see a yolk sac inside the amniotic sac, which is the embryo that will grow into a fetus.

- ◆ **Gestational sac:** A sac filled with fluid that surrounds an embryo in the early stages of pregnancy.[2]
- ◆ **Amniotic sac:** A smaller, thinner sac that forms between the embryo/fetus and the gestational sac in early pregnancy.
- ◆ **Yolk sac:** Also known as an *umbilical vesicle,* a yolk sac is seen in the earliest stages of pregnancy and plays a crucial role in the

development of an embryo into a fetus. Throughout the later part of the first trimester, it will start to regress and no longer be needed. Some physicians have said that it plays a role in the development of the placenta.[3]

◆ **Fetal pole:** Found next to the yolk sac and said to look like a "grain of rice," this is an embryo that is growing into the fetus stage of development. A fetal pole is needed in order to measure a pregnancy and to see cardiac activity.

PREGNANCY VIABILITY

Now that I've discussed the anatomy of pregnancy in general and what you can see on an early ultrasound, this section discusses what makes a pregnancy viable versus one that isn't viable. Again, the terminology can add to the grief because we tend to question why and end up without answers to these questions. It's completely valid to be upset over the terms of pregnancy and loss because your pregnancy loss experience is personal.

A *viable pregnancy* is one that continues to grow and thrive without any concerns over its ability to survive outside of the woman's body. Sometimes this isn't necessarily known or discussed unless there's a concern. However, a viable pregnancy can still end in loss, which I understand is a bit confusing. When the pregnancy itself is healthy, free of genetic conditions that can hinder life, and able to grow and thrive in a womb, it is considered viable. However, if someone were to go into premature labor or have early loss of their amniotic fluid causing an earlier than planned labor, loss can still happen. Therefore, viable, sadly, still doesn't mean that someone ends that pregnancy with a baby in their arms.

An *unviable* or *non-viable pregnancy* is often determined early in the pregnancy itself. Most commonly it is diagnosed during the first, possibly the second, ultrasound. It can also be determined following genetic testing or during the anatomy scan ultrasound, however, that's less likely. What this means is that the pregnancy will likely not be able to survive outside of the woman's body and the pregnancy itself will most likely end with a loss of some kind. Medically, this may be referred to as a *threatened abortion*. In my work, I often call this *pregnancy limbo* and refer to it as a terrible position to be in. Sometimes people with diagnoses that indicate a pregnancy is unviable may opt for a version of termination for medical reasons, which I also discuss in the next section.

During pregnancy, there is a milestone referred to as the *viability week,* which is at 24 weeks of pregnancy. What this means is that medically, a baby should have a good chance at surviving outside of the pregnant person's body. If premature labor were to happen at 24 weeks of pregnancy, your medical team would be able to attempt lifesaving measures on your baby. Although birth at this point would result in a lengthy hospital stay and possible long-term health complications, odds are good that the baby would survive. Actually, in the medical field, they do lifesaving measures as early as 22 weeks.

Of course, in writing about the viability milestone, loss is still very possible even when a baby is born after this 24-week milestone. There may be someone reading this book who has experienced premature labor and the death of their child—as I try to point out in everything I teach and discuss, pregnancy loss or neonatal loss can happen in the blink of an eye. It's scary to think of and horrible to know that people experience this type of death, but being aware of it only shows us where to go if it happens to us.

It doesn't matter what type of loss you experience or what your views are on reproductive health, pregnancy loss is incredibly difficult on every level. When I'm working with a client to process their pregnancy loss experience, a huge focus is making sure they understand what happened but also that they did everything they could. Sometimes, doing all we can do isn't enough to prevent the loss, but it is enough to focus our grief on the loss itself instead of suffering feelings of self-blame.

- ◆ **Viable pregnancy:** A pregnancy that results in a baby that can survive outside of the pregnant person's body.

♦ **Unviable pregnancy:** A pregnancy that is unlikely to continue in utero and will likely result in pregnancy loss of some kind.

Another term that you may hear used is *recurrent pregnancy loss*. There is a lot of confusion surrounding this topic and the diagnosis itself. This term comes from the American Society for Reproductive Medicine (ASRM),[4] which often sets the precedent for things that affect reproductive health. By definition *recurrent pregnancy loss* is when someone experiences two or more miscarriages or types of pregnancy loss. Over time, the definition has evolved to be what we have today, which is inclusive to most types of loss.

The definition of recurrent pregnancy loss used to refer to the loss of three or more subsequent pregnancies and did not have exceptions for ectopic or chemical pregnancies. Luckily in recent years, this definition has shifted to match the needs of women and now speaks for two or more subsequent pregnancy losses and does include ectopic pregnancy as well as chemical pregnancies.

You may be wondering why this is important information. Recurrent losses are devastating regardless of how they are categorized or defined. The reason why they are a big deal is because in the United States specifically, is that being diagnosed with this condition can affect healthcare coverage for medical care and testing. To get a diagnosis code for recurrent pregnancy loss, you must fall under the clinical definition. This creates problems for people in other countries because their government gets to decide what is covered (or when something is covered), so many countries, such as Canada and the United Kingdom, have continued to follow the old guidelines of three or more losses. Of course, there's always wiggle room, and people are still finding ways to get access to this care, but it's a complicated process.

As someone who has experienced two miscarriages and who supports thousands of people who are navigating this experience, I feel like I can speak to why recurrent loss feels so different than having a single loss.

It's never that those with one loss have a less valid experience, it's that there's a mind shift that happens after a second miscarriage.

When you have one miscarriage, medical providers or people close to you might say, oh it's so common, it won't happen next time. When a second (or third or fourth) miscarriage happens, many women tend to feel broken. It's when they wonder what's wrong with them and it's incredibly isolating.

Language Is Important

Although pregnancy loss can bring people together through support groups and online communities, each experience is deeply personal. We may connect with others' stories and find comfort in shared experiences, yet our loss remains uniquely our own because it happened to and within our body.

Language is such an important piece of moving forward through grief. Pregnancy loss is a hot-button topic. There are many types of loss to experience, emotions that people feel, and differences in how it's discussed. As a bereavement doula, I focus on meeting people where they are in grief and asking questions that other people don't feel comfortable bringing up.

Such as the term *miscarriage*.

At baseline, the word is terrible and I'll tell you why. To imply that someone can miscarry their pregnancy, meaning not to carry properly or well, is hurtful. Of course, most people who experience pregnancy loss these days know that it's a societal term and it isn't to be taken literally—but it still hurts. Many of my clients agree that the word itself is hard to say and it's hard to hear when others are discussing pregnancy loss. But what's difficult with the language surrounding the loss of a pregnancy is that there are almost too many layers, too many options, and too many reasons why all of the terminology is painfully outdated.

Miscarriage is a term that's often used when someone experiences pregnancy loss before 20 weeks' gestation. The term *stillbirth* is used for losses that occur after the 20-week mark. Under the umbrella of those terms are a variety of sub-terms used to describe the different types of loss. It's complicated to properly grieve when we have terminology that makes us feel invalidated. Medical terms are sprinkled in and then if we dare to search the Internet for the meaning behind the words used to describe our devastating loss, we can end up feeling even worse.

A DEATH HAS OCCURRED

So, let's call it what it is—a death.

A death has occurred and how it happened is only relevant in processing what you've gone through and how your loss may be treated. But no matter what term is used—you're grieving the death of a life. You've experienced a death and that's a lot to cope with even if you have all the tools.

The vast majority of pregnancy loss is completely out of the control of the pregnant person. Even so, many women feel a sense of blame or guilt. It's hard to pinpoint why that is, but the language itself often implies some kind of personal failure. Neither you nor that life was a failure. Life is fragile and this is a devastatingly painful way to learn of that fragility.

People may have a preference on how they discuss their pregnancy loss, which is why I point out how important it is to discuss language and make sure everyone is on the same page. There's a debate in the online miscarriage community and that often revolves around using the terms miscarriage or pregnancy loss. Which are correct?

Throughout this book, I use different terms related to pregnancy loss interchangeably because I want you to feel seen and represented in each chapter. Working with people who are navigating pregnancy loss at 5 weeks, 10 weeks, 15 weeks, 28 weeks, and beyond—I know that the language is deeply personal. In many ways I find it unfair that we don't have more specific language that fits the needs of everyone.

A loss at eight weeks' gestation is treated differently, medically, than a loss at 17 weeks' gestation. However, through the eyes of society, both are called a miscarriage. I preach on social media that comparison is the thief of grief because we should never think that someone has it worse, so we shouldn't be sad. Or use that comparison as a tool to force us forward. Human beings have different lived experiences and that's just the way it is. In finding support through pregnancy loss, it's important to find people with similar experiences. Similar experiences often lead to similar emotions and that's why, in my practice, I don't just have support groups for miscarriage and force all gestations together. I do what I can to provide space dependent on many factors, such as the trimester in which the loss happened, whether this was a first pregnancy or if it's recurrent losses, and if someone has living children prior to their loss. All of these details impact how we discuss loss, how we process the experience itself, and how we find community.

Again, that's why I refer to it as death.

MEDICAL TERMINOLOGY CAN BE HURTFUL

Language can be difficult to navigate, especially when the medical terminology doesn't match how we feel about pregnancy loss. In the medical field, pregnancy loss at any gestation is often referred to as an *abortion*, which is upsetting for many people no matter where their political alliances are. The truth is that there aren't separate medical terms for pregnancy loss that separates loss by the intention of the pregnancy. Some of the medical terms are spontaneous abortion, threatened abortion, pregnancy with abortive outcome, and complete abortion. And of course, there are people in the loss community who have what's called a termination for medical reasons, which you can read more about in the glossary. Let's break down what this means. That way you can cope with your loss and avoid this trigger as you navigate life after loss.

When medical professionals diagnose a miscarriage—no matter if it's an OB-GYN (obstetrician/gynecologist), nurse practitioner, fertility doctor, or family doctor—they use the medical word abortion because of the treatment for pregnancy loss.

Using my own experience with a missed miscarriage as an example, I learned that my pregnancy had stopped growing at six weeks even though I should have been 11 weeks along. When this was confirmed, I was given three options: wait for the miscarriage to happen on its own, induce the physical miscarriage using medication, or have a procedure such as a D&C (*dilation and curettage*). These are the same protocols used for pregnancies that are terminated for whatever reason. Our medical system uses something called ICD codes, which helps medical providers code the services they provide so that insurance companies can file it away as covered or not covered. Plus, these codes provide cash pricing and are used to keep medical records of diagnoses. Prior to experiencing pregnancy loss, most people are completely unaware of how the system works.

In another life, 10+ years ago, I worked as a medical assistant. Part of my job description was providing ICD codes to insurance companies and helping patients get services covered. Therefore, I've seen the importance of the coding system. However, being a patient, especially when suffering a miscarriage, I was unprepared for the emotional toll of seeing the word abortion on my medical forms. Many doctors wisely refrain from referring to a treated miscarriage as an abortion so the only time this usually comes up is when referring to coding.

Another piece of language that I find to be important is the topic surrounding motherhood in general. This often affects those who have lost their first pregnancy and do not have living children prior to loss. I'll sit with clients as they focus on their grief and trauma and ask them if they feel like a mother. The question itself is an emotional one and I believe that's because no one asks it. It's too uncomfortable to think that a mother has lost their child. But that is what has happened to many people.

Amy—a client of mine whose name I've changed for privacy—experienced what's called a chemical pregnancy. She felt conflicted. She had friends who experienced early losses, and she never thought of it as more than losing a pregnancy; she didn't understand why others would be so distraught over a pregnancy that didn't grow longer than a few days. Then she had the firsthand experience that changed her life forever. From the moment the pregnancy test was positive, she felt that love and connection for the little life growing inside of her, and she saw that life as her baby. Then she started bleeding, only two days after the positive pregnancy test, and she felt immediate sorrow for the life that she was losing. In just two days, Amy had made plans and had dreams. She thought of how she would decorate the nursery. There were images in her head of how life would look with a baby in her arms, and it brought her so much joy. But then she started bleeding and the second line on the pregnancy test faded. Now that future was empty and so was Amy.

Even with an early loss, the grief is all-consuming and it seems that it often surprises people. The professional side of me wants to say it's because society has conditioned us to not see pregnancy loss as a big deal. But humans are complicated and have a lot of emotions—often at once—which can be overwhelming, so we shut some of those big emotions out and try to ignore them. Does this sound familiar?

Amy and I had a one-on-one support session and discussed terminology at length. She expressed that she used to refer to her friend's pregnancy loss as a chemical pregnancy because she had heard the term used before and based on her quick Internet search, that's what it was called in different articles and on websites. But now that she had experienced the same loss as that friend, she found the term offensive and invalidating of the life that she and her partner had created together. Amy decided that saying "miscarriage" was more comfortable. There's no gestation point where the pain becomes more valid than another. Amy had a miscarriage, and she was devastated. End of story.

Reflection Prompts

I encourage you to take a moment and reflect on the following questions about language.

- ◆ Do you relate to the sentiment of losing a baby or do you feel as though you've lost a pregnancy?
- ◆ Does saying "I had a miscarriage" properly encompass the experience you've had? If not, which phrasing do you prefer?
- ◆ If you've experienced pregnancy loss in the second trimester, what language feels best when talking about the loss of your baby?
- ◆ Some people struggle with the thought of "losing" their baby because they aren't lost, they died. How do you feel about this phrasing?
- ◆ [For those without living children] Do you feel as though you're a mother?

Types of Pregnancy Loss

Having a miscarriage is not a cut-and-dry experience; there are many ways for pregnancy loss to occur. Even though there are only a few medical terms used to describe a loss, there are a dozen or so different terms used to recognize specific types of loss. This section delves into these types of loss.

MISSED MISCARRIAGE

A missed miscarriage is a term that's used to describe a type of pregnancy loss that occurs with no physical signs of a miscarriage happening. It's often diagnosed during the first ultrasound, when the pregnancy is determined as behind the gestational age based on the pregnant person's last menstrual period and/or if there's no cardiac activity.

These losses can actually occur anytime between 6–20 weeks (after 20 weeks, it would more likely be referred to as a stillbirth). No matter the gestation, a missed miscarriage (or missed pregnancy loss) is diagnosed or confirmed the same way—by ultrasound.

A few examples of people learning about a missed miscarriage may look like these:

- Emily went into her anatomy scan ultrasound at 20 weeks pregnant to learn that her baby had died during the 18th week. She wouldn't necessarily be expected to feel movement yet; she didn't have any bleeding; and she had a doppler check at her 16th week appointment where everything was okay.
- Tamra goes to her fertility clinic for the first ultrasound to check on her IVF pregnancy at seven weeks pregnant. During the ultrasound, there is no cardiac activity, the gestational sac is measuring a few days behind, and the doctor says that they don't like what they see but cannot be sure if the pregnancy is viable or not. Tamra and her partner are told to return for another ultrasound in 10 days, when the doctor will check for growth and determine if it's a viable pregnancy.

Treatment for a missed miscarriage varies, because people are often given a set of options, which are all equally difficult. One unique aspect of a missed miscarriage is that the body hasn't started to go into labor on its own, so it clearly either needs more time or some medical assistance. As a miscarriage doula, I worry about the safety of my clients with missed miscarriages. Processing that your baby has died or that your pregnancy is ending and then having to make informed decisions to navigate what comes next is near impossible. It's a lot to take on and there's so much happening at once, which is why having resources and community is so important.

SPONTANEOUS MISCARRIAGE

A spontaneous miscarriage is a completely different type of miscarriage. As the term suggests, this type of loss is spontaneous and usually happens with some warning, but it can also happen without any warning at all. For some, spotting will begin and then turn into heavier bleeding, which indicates a miscarriage. Then they give physical birth in the first or early second trimester. Others might experience a sensation of their water breaking (many report feeling a popping sensation), which is followed by what I call an untimely home birth.

BLIGHTED OVUM

Possibly the most confusing type of miscarriage is a blighted ovum. By definition, a blighted ovum is when an embryo stops developing before cardiac activity and is often considered to be under the missed miscarriage umbrella. Most people who receive this diagnosis learn about their loss during the first or second ultrasound, when the pregnancy is measuring 5–6 weeks and doesn't have a heartbeat.

Something that's very difficult about a blighted ovum is how medical professionals tend to discuss this loss with patients. We hear a lot of words such as empty, or nothing is there. Emotionally, that can be very damaging.

Let's be clear about one thing—when you have a blighted ovum, you are pregnant. Without a doubt, you are pregnant. The pregnancy doesn't disappear or become invalidated because the growth stopped in the early stages. Your grief and any trauma associated with pregnancy loss are valid.

Instead, I tend to focus on how unfair or unfortunate it is to experience loss without knowing if your baby had a heartbeat or without getting to hear a heartbeat like others might get to.

CHEMICAL PREGNANCY

As a miscarriage doula who focuses on grief and trauma, I loathe the term chemical pregnancy because I find that it diminishes so much of people's experiences with early pregnancy loss. But this wouldn't be an inclusive pregnancy loss guide without discussing chemical pregnancies. This term is used often in a medical setting and it trickles into society.

I always try to make it clear that I, personally and professionally, consider this type of pregnancy and loss to be a spontaneous and early type of pregnancy loss. From the outside, this might seem like the better option among miscarriages, but I assure you that the grief is still real. A chemical pregnancy or chemical miscarriage is often used to describe a pregnancy that ends prior to five- or six-weeks' gestation. More commonly, this type of miscarriage happens within days of finding out about a pregnancy. In many cases, someone will take a home pregnancy test or receive blood work results and learn that their levels are low (or a faint positive on a home test) and the number will continue to fall, or the test will go from positive to negative. This specific type of loss happens quickly and often causes the pregnant person to feel invalidated in their grief, confused by what's happened, and then not acknowledged by others. While the term isn't a medical term, medical providers will use this explanation for loss to make someone feel better about their miscarriage (it often doesn't).

I often meet with clients who share that they've had early losses and the way they phrase it is usually something along the lines of, "It doesn't count but I had a chemical pregnancy." Which I always respond to by letting them know that it does count, it does matter, and they should still take the time to mourn their loss.

I had a client, I'll call her Melissa, who suffered four chemical pregnancies. When I sat down to talk with her, she broke down crying because she felt silly for reaching out for support over pregnancies that lasted a matter of days. It was heartbreaking to see, because clearly her grief and loss was real, regardless of the gestation of those pregnancies.

Society likes to remind us that miscarriages are common, they are normal, and that you will move on. That messaging gets stuck when it comes to these early losses because then we think about how someone, somewhere has it far worse than us. Then, we tend to gaslight ourselves into thinking that our experience and grief really isn't that big of a deal. But the truth is that this type of loss causes a lot of devastation, confusion, fear, and so on.

One thing that is difficult and unique about early losses that are categorized as chemical pregnancies is that some people learn about their pregnancy and loss after the fact. An example of this is if someone has a period that is 1–2 days late and it's a tad heavier than usual, and bloodwork or a home pregnancy test may show low HCG levels (a pregnancy hormone) indicating that they were pregnant and had a miscarriage. For clients who have experienced that very example, they often feel guilty for not testing sooner so they could know for sure that they were pregnant. They struggle to know what to think about this type of loss. Don't let the name of this type of loss fool you—it's more than chemicals, it is an embryo, and its worthy of grief too.

In 2017, my husband and I had been trying to conceive for a few months, and I was becoming really concerned about my fertility health. Then I had this cycle that was so confusing and concerning, so I made an appointment with my OB-GYN to discuss. I was a part of some Facebook groups, I had a fertility blog, I was surrounded by this self-made community, and the feedback I was receiving made me feel uneasy.

I took a cheap home pregnancy test. To this day, I swear that I saw a second line which indicated a pregnancy existing. But every person I shared a photo with (of the pregnancy test) would tell me that it was negative and gave me the impression that they were worried about my mental well-being while trying to conceive. As though I was this sad, poor infertile girl who wanted to be pregnant so bad that she would hallucinate and see a faint second line on this pregnancy test. In my gut, I knew that I wasn't wrong, but I also wasn't sure that I was pregnant, which I understand will make little sense to most people. When I went and saw my doctor, I showed her the photos, I told her that I had been spotting and that my periods didn't line up. It was as though I had a period a week earlier than usual and now the pregnancy tests were negative. She explained to me that she could draw blood work and measure my beta HCG, but that ultimately, it sounded like a chemical pregnancy.

In all honesty, I pushed that experience far back into my mind and never counted that as a pregnancy loss because of how confusing the timeline was and how unsure I felt about the pregnancy test. To this day, I swear it was faintly positive for a single day. Once I started The Miscarriage Doula, I found a lot of healing in my own experience because I met people with very similar experiences and realized just how much empathy I felt for them.

A few examples of chemical pregnancy experiences may look like these:

◆ Callie takes a home pregnancy test on a Monday and it's clearly posi-tive. On Wednesday she has some spotting but isn't concerned as she knows that can sometimes happen during pregnancy. By Friday, the bleeding is more period-like and she now has cramping. She decides to take a home pregnancy test for reassurance that every-thing is okay but is confused when her digital pregnancy test now comes back negative. She calls her doctor who has her come in for two rounds of blood work which confirms that her HCG (a preg-nancy hormone test by blood) levels are low and continuing to decline. She's had a chemical miscarriage (according to the definition).

◆ Abby and her partner did IVF to get pregnant, and they had their first beta on a Wednesday. A beta HCG represents the beta subunit that is often tested through blood work. The results are in numeric form and gives doctors a good idea on how the pregnancy is progressing early in pregnancy. In Abby's case, the HCG level comes back at 60 and she celebrates this win. When she returns to the clinic on Friday or her second blood work, she learns that her level is only 85. While this number is higher than the first, it's not the standard 40% rise, which is concerning. A third beta is done on Monday, and her num-ber is now 93. Her doctor has instructed her to stop all her IVF medi-cations in hopes that the miscarriage will occur on its own (since these medications can interfere with pregnancy). She does as told and within 36 hours, she starts bleeding. This is considered a chemical pregnancy.

ECTOPIC PREGNANCY

An *ectopic* pregnancy is a potentially life-threatening type of pregnancy where the embryo has attached itself to someplace outside of the uterus. The placement is generally in one of the fallopian tubes but can also be attached on the cusp of the fallopian tube, where it flows into the uterus. If someone has had a previous cesarean section delivery, it can attach to the scar tissue, which can also cause life-threatening outcomes.

There are many difficult aspects of an ectopic pregnancy. One being that symptoms can vary from person to person and it's not rare that someone doesn't know they are experiencing an ectopic pregnancy until they are in extreme pain and in need of immediate medical care. A lot of women will feel hopeless or lost after experiencing this type of loss because they question how well they know their body or if they are able to carry a pregnancy in their uterus. Even when they know that they aren't at fault, there's an amount of self-blame that occurs. It's difficult to cope with a pregnancy that couldn't have survived even if the embryo was healthy, but would have resulted in a living child if it had implanted in the correct placement. It's a painful reality for thousands of people each year.

One question that people often have about ectopic pregnancies is how they are treated. Since it's known that a pregnancy cannot survive outside of the uterus, what's done for someone who is experiencing one of these pregnancies? Unfortunately, a termination for medical reasons is necessary. A specific medication is often used, called methotrexate, which is an injection that essentially ends the pregnancy. The injection is given and then oftentimes there is an amount of bleeding that follows and the person is then told to trend their beta HCG levels to ensure that the pregnancy has ended and left the body. If the levels remain high or don't go down below five on their own, another dose of the medication might be necessary.

Depending on the gestational age and level of intensity, surgery might be required. There can also be a mandatory waiting period before trying to get pregnant again, which can feel like another gut punch. Coping with the loss of a pregnancy, the unlucky placement of that pregnancy, and being told you can't do something—it's a lot to process.

A few examples of ectopic pregnancy experiences may look like these:

- Lindsey learns that she's pregnant and requests a beta HCG blood draw from her doctor. It starts to show an abnormal rise in HCG levels, which raises some concern. By following the HCG levels and doing ultrasounds around five weeks (1.5–2 weeks after the first blood draw), they learn that the pregnancy is not in the uterus and suspect that it's in a fallopian tube. Because the levels are low enough not to raise medical concern and not high enough for the pregnancy to be more than five weeks along, it's recommended that Lindsey take methotrexate, which should terminate the pregnancy and help it leave her body.

- Paige is eight weeks pregnant and notices some cramping in her lower abdomen on the left side. She has her first ultrasound in one week. After a few days, the cramping turns into a more intense pain that makes it difficult to stand or complete her daily activities. She calls her OB-GYN's office, and they urge her to go to the emergency room. Paige does go to the ER and learns that she's experiencing an ectopic pregnancy. The pregnancy is in the left fallopian tube but the tube has not ruptured. Due to her pain and discomfort, it's recommended that she have surgery to ensure the ectopic pregnancy is properly treated.

MOLAR AND PARTIAL-MOLAR PREGNANCY

A molar pregnancy is a rare type of pregnancy loss where essentially a specific type of mole, called a *hydatidiform mole,* grows because of a complication that happens genetically at conception. There are two types of molar pregnancies: a complete molar pregnancy or a partial molar pregnancy.

It's important to know that these pregnancies are not viable and there's unfortunately nothing anyone can do to prevent them. While that doesn't erase grief felt, it can help to settle the mind and ease the self-blame that someone experiencing one might feel.

STILLBIRTH

Prior to 20 weeks of pregnancy, you'll often hear pregnancy loss referred to as a miscarriage. Once someone reaches 20 weeks and experiences a loss, it's referred to as stillbirth. The terminology itself is tricky because someone might not identify with any of these terms. It's personal and sometimes the terms cause more grief. For example, if someone experiences the death of their unborn child at 17 weeks of pregnancy, learning that their heart had stopped one week prior, at 16 weeks—they might not identify with the term miscarriage. That's okay—this type of pregnancy loss is personal and the support given to people who have experienced stillbirth might blend into support given during second trimester pregnancy loss altogether.

There is no single reason why stillbirths happen and, unfortunately, most people think that they are in the "safe zone" once they reach the second trimester and therefore this type of loss is a shock.

A few of the causes of pregnancy loss after 20 weeks may be due to an undiagnosed genetic condition, racial disparity, umbilical cord incidents, placental growth restrictions, infections, or maternal health conditions. Using up-to-date and current technology could prevent at least 25% of stillbirths that happen today but, just like first trimester loss, we don't know what to advocate for until we've, unfortunately, been through it. It's the most painful way to learn something.

But let me be clear—parents are not at fault for stillbirth. Even if we discuss some reasons that are preventable, there are factors involved that put us at a higher risk of not being in a position to have the care necessary to prevent these losses.

The racial disparity of good maternal healthcare is one cause of stillbirth that we could change, and they make up roughly 27% of all cases of still-born children.[5] This is why women of color twice are likely to have a still-birth than a white female.

You may be wondering how we can change this. How can we ensure that we are advocating for ourselves in pregnancy? How can healthcare work-ers help women of color feel safer?

As a patient, the best thing you can do is advocate for yourself. For exam-ple, if your baby's movement feels off or weird and you can't explain it other than it's a bad feeling, demand to be seen. Demand an ultrasound, ask them to check on your placenta, check on your cervix, or even swab you for infections. There are never too many requests that you can make when you are pregnant because all you're trying to do is ensure the safety of yourself and your unborn child.

To support women of color, especially if you work in the medical field, the first step is to listen to them. Listen to their pain, their discomfort, and their questions. We should all be treated, respected, and heard.

A few examples of stillbirth experiences may look like these:

- ◆ Amanda has been going in for extra growth ultrasounds because her daughter has measured small over the last eight weeks. She's cur-rently 39 weeks pregnant and feeling a decrease in movement, so she calls her OB-GYN, who tells her to go to Labor & Delivery. She learns while at the hospital that her daughter's heart is no longer beating and that she possibly died within the last 24 hours. Amanda now must attempt to give vaginal birth to a baby that has a room, a name, and was loved, wanted, and cared for. Later she learns that her placenta was too small to support the baby and her daughter died from that complication. This could have been caught sooner by measuring her placenta and scheduling an earlier delivery while also monitoring the baby.

◆ Sarah goes in for her anatomy scan at 21 weeks pregnant and is excited because she hasn't seen the baby since she was 10 weeks pregnant, as that's the usual protocol at this office. She last heard the baby's heartbeat on the doppler at her appointment four weeks prior to her anatomy scan. During the ultrasound, the technician becomes quiet and then shares that she cannot find a heartbeat, and it looks like the baby stopped growing two weeks before. Sarah then goes to the hospital, where she is induced and gives birth to her baby, who is no longer alive. With testing, she learns that her baby had Trisomy 13, a genetic condition that is not compatible with life. It's possible that this could have been caught by an earlier ultrasound or by doing NIPT (non-invasive prenatal testing). This would not have prevented the death of her child but would have prepared her for this death or given her options earlier than 21 weeks of pregnancy.

TERMINATION FOR MEDICAL REASONS

A unique, yet important, type of pregnancy loss is when someone is pregnant and is advised to or requests to terminate their pregnancy for medical reasons. These medical reasons can be for one of many reasons, such as maternal mental health, genetic conditions, developmental conditions, high-risk pregnancy, or harm to the pregnant person. Someone also may have a pregnancy with multiples (two or more babies) and wish to reduce the number of babies in their uterus.

Often abbreviated as TFMR, it may often seem like a choice, but it's a compassionate one that doesn't often feel like a choice to the person going through it.

These losses are of children—babies—that are incredibly wanted and loved by their parent(s). Plus, the process of termination is never an easy thing to navigate. It often leaves the family with trauma, grief, blame, and then guilt when adding the social stigmas and political opinions.

A few examples of termination for medical reasons experiences may look like these:

- ◆ Bethany is pregnant and at 11 weeks' gestation, she has NIPT testing done to check for genetic abnormalities. A few weeks after the blood test is performed, she gets a phone call from her doctor who shares that Bethany's baby has Turner's Syndrome, which is often not compatible with life. The doctor gives her options to do more invasive testing (such as a CVS or amniocentesis) to properly diagnose this condition. A CVS (chorionic villus sampling) procedure involves testing a sample of the placental tissue during the second trimester to rule out genetic abnormalities. By the time Bethany has the CVS test performed and receives the results that her child does in fact have a severe diagnosis of Turner's Syndrome, she is 16 weeks pregnant. She and her partner then take two weeks to decide how they would like to move forward. At 18 weeks, she decides to have a termination for medical reasons.

- ◆ Alex is pregnant with triplets and is advised to consider reducing the number of fetuses to two or one due to a concern for her physical well-being and other preexisting conditions that make her high risk with one pregnancy. Having a pregnancy of multiples is concerning her doctor so they get a second and third opinion—all of which suggest a termination of one fetus. Alex goes through with the reduction at 17 weeks pregnant and goes on to have two healthy children after struggling with gestational diabetes and pre-eclampsia.

VANISHING TWIN SYNDROME

Dr. Zarlakhta Zamani explains Vanishing Twin Syndrome as "a condition in which one of a set of twins or multiple embryos dies in utero, disappears, or gets resorbed partially or entirely, with an outcome of a spontaneous reduction of a multi-fetus pregnancy to a singleton pregnancy, portraying the image of a vanishing twin."[6]

Experiencing the loss of one pregnancy while continuing to carry another pregnancy is often described as confusing and the people who have these losses tend to not fully process the loss itself until after the surviving child is born. It's a complicated type of loss, not that any of these losses are easy, and is often overlooked when including people who have experienced loss.

Being diagnosed with a vanishing twin often happens early in pregnancy, during the first trimester, but can happen later as well.

A few examples of vanishing twin syndrome experiences may look like these:

◆ At six weeks pregnant, Stella goes in for an early first ultrasound because she previously experienced a missed miscarriage at 10 weeks. During this ultrasound, the doctor sees that there are two gestational sacs and only one sac currently has cardiac activity. Stella is told to come back in one week to review the progress of the pregnancy. One week later, Stella returns to her doctor's office and the ultrasound reveals that the gestational sac that had cardiac activity has grown and is measuring two days ahead but, sadly, the other sack hasn't grown at all and has appeared to shrink in size. Stella is diagnosed with a vanishing twin. When she's checked again at 10 weeks, it's confirmed without uncertainty.

◆ Lila is pregnant with twins and goes in for an ultrasound at 16 weeks to learn that one of her twins has died and that their growth stopped at 13 weeks' gestation. She is told that she may not have any bleeding and that the baby will shrink and absorb into her gestational sac over the course of the remainder of her pregnancy. Due to this loss, technicians are careful in future ultrasounds to ensure that Lila doesn't see the child that is no longer alive and at birth, the same care is given.

PPROM (PRETERM PREMATURE RUPTURE OF MEMBRANES)

PPROM is categorized as premature birth in most instances or a loss that happens during the second or third trimester. This happens when someone is leaking amniotic fluid, or has suddenly lost fluid, which may cause them to go into labor. While it's possible for someone to have PPROM and for their child to survive, there are a lot of factors at play and, sadly, a good outcome is unlikely with this diagnosis.

As you can tell from these types of pregnancy loss, there are many ways that someone can experience loss.

Treatment Options for Pregnancy Loss

At the time of being told that you're experiencing a miscarriage or that your baby doesn't have a heartbeat, your brain cannot properly take in the options that are given to you. And in some cases, people aren't given options because their doctor recommends one route, or their loss happens very quickly (or spontaneously).

Through The Miscarriage Doula, I've met countless women who reported feeling numb in those moments. They mention that they just couldn't take in the information laid out for them. It's unfortunately a justified response because you are essentially in a state of shock. Also, the options are given to us in some of the most basic terms where even if we could take on that information, I'm not sure that our medical system properly lays out all of the information for us. What's the right answer? How can someone make an informed decision at that moment? As someone who has felt that shock firsthand and made poor decisions based on the numbness that came with learning I was having a miscarriage, I can tell you that there's no right answer.

When it comes to pregnancy loss, every option is horrible and sad. There's no way to bypass the difficulties of loss and it's the unfortunate truth of the matter. If you're reading this and seeking some sort of backup to the voice in your head that tells you that you made a mistake in whatever option you chose, you won't find that here. You did what was best for you during a difficult moment. An impossible moment.

I am here to validate that every option is hard, while also providing you with information on each option. That way you can understand it better (even if it's after the fact) or have the information to share with someone you love if they have to navigate loss.

If you have the ability to choose which avenue of pregnancy loss you're going to experience, then it's important to sit with the options and choose what feels best for you. While some options have more "horror" stories than others, they are all difficult. We often try to bypass the trauma or go for whichever seems safest but when it comes to this type of loss, it's impossible to choose a "better" option because they are all unfortunate options.

When it comes to experiencing pregnancy loss, every outcome is a sad one. It's all untimely and unfair—there's no redemption in the fact that this pregnancy isn't viable. Even if you know exactly why this was happening to you, it is still difficult to physically experience a loss like this.

In the following sections, I discuss some different options or types of physical loss. My hope is that you'll feel more informed, which will help process your experience while knowing that you can be a resource for someone else in your life if they have a miscarriage. In this community,

I also find that people will want to have a *disaster relief plan* in case they have further loss, too.

FIRST TRIMESTER: HAVING YOUR MISCARRIAGE AT HOME, UNMEDICATED

Having a miscarriage at home without any intervention means that your body goes through the labor process and essentially gives birth without medication to start the process. This is when your pregnancy leaves your body and physical healing may begin. People who experience the physical element of pregnancy loss in this way either were given a choice to "wait it out" and allow their body to go through the necessary stages of labor in the first trimester, or experienced a spontaneous miscarriage without any warning or choice. Both avenues of physical loss are incredibly difficult.

While we know the general timeline and expectations that occur when someone has a miscarriage at home, there are elements of pregnancy loss that we can't predict or know for certain. Just like there's no blueprint for grief, there's no guarantee that miscarriage will look one specific way. Some people may have a seemingly "okay" experience, while others leave their physical loss with additional trauma from the pain and intensity.

The physical experience of pregnancy loss is a spectrum. The best-case scenario is that the bleeding is a little heavier than a usual period, that the pain is manageable with Motrin, and that you are comfortable and safe. A worst-case scenario is that you bleed extremely heavily—filling 1–2 pads within an hour—have intense cramping and contractions, feel faint, can't keep liquids or food down, and need medical care.

When a miscarriage happens at home, whether it's expected or a shock, it may begin with spotting and/or cramping before the physical labor begins. Oftentimes, if someone is experiencing a missed miscarriage and they have been spotting during their pregnancy, it could be a good indicator that the physical miscarriage will take place soon. Some women will bleed in small amounts, such as spotting, for days or weeks before what I refer to as "the worst of it" happens. If someone is later in their pregnancy, somewhere between 11–20 weeks, then they may not have spotting. Those people could have cramping, but write it off to be normal pregnancy cramping, then feel a pop sensation that is followed by labor. Just like there are many different types of pregnancy loss, there are various ways that someone can experience physical labor.

FIRST TRIMESTER: TAKING INDUCTION MEDICATIONS AND HAVING THE MISCARRIAGE AT HOME

Medication management for a miscarriage usually happens when pregnancy loss occurs prior to the 14th week of pregnancy. Although it's based on the doctor's recommendation, many doctors recommend a D&C if you experience a loss at the beginning of the second trimester. There are a lot of factors that go into this option of treatment.

If you're located in the United States, this option may look different based on the state you live in. There are two medications used for induction and in some states, only one medication is legal for use due to abortion laws by state. In some countries, this option can be completed at home or in a medical setting like a hospital.

One of the medications is a progesterone blocker and the other is a medication that softens your cervix and induces contractions, which helps the physical miscarriage take place. Together, the success rates are believed to be higher without as many complications. In states where the progesterone blocker isn't legal anymore, there's a higher rate of complications from the cervical dilation and contraction inducer medication. One thing to know about this option is that the induction medication that's given after the progesterone blocker is also used in the delivery of a full-term pregnancy. The main difference is that for pregnancy loss, the dosage is three to four times higher than what's used for a live birth. Therefore, your body is working in overdrive to birth your first trimester pregnancy; this can be very painful.

Through many studies that have been completed on the use of these medications, roughly 78% of women who use them have success, which means they have their complete miscarriage and do not need surgical care.[7]

It's important to know that a portion of the people who take the medication with the hopes of it being successful do find themselves taking multiple doses over many weeks or having a D&C (Dilation and Curettage) or D&E (Dilation and Evacuation). How *well* the medication works is unpredictable so it's important to be aware of the possibility.

FIRST TRIMESTER: HAVING A PROCEDURE SUCH AS A D&C

A misconception related to the options of treatment with pregnancy loss is that there is an easy way out. Oftentimes, there is a rhetoric that having a procedure is a quick way out of experiencing a physical miscarriage. There's a similar thought process with full-term deliveries and those who have cesarean sections although that's not true either. We have to acknowledge that birth at any time, at any gestational age, and with whatever assistance (or lack thereof) is difficult, painful, and life altering.

During the first trimester the more common procedure is a D&C, which means *dilation and curettage*. It's generally a surgical procedure that is performed in the operating room while under general anesthesia.

There are variations of procedures that can be done when someone has had a miscarriage, and they may be referred to under different names. Another procedure that may occur is a D&E which means *dilation and evacuation*. The main difference between a D&C and a D&E is the tools used. With a D&E, someone may be awake, and they could be unmedicated; however, that's not recommended. Another variation of this procedure is a D&C except with aspiration used. This type of D&C can be performed in a doctor's office rather than an OR and it's advised to be under some pain medication instead of under anesthesia.

Often, when women are explained their options, it's made simple by just mentioning the D&C and performing the procedure in an operating room

(OR). Depending on the gestational age of the pregnancy, the financial status of the family, and other factors expressed by the pregnant person, there are other options available.

FIRST TRIMESTER: ECTOPIC PREGNANCY AND TAKING METHOTREXATE

Ectopic pregnancy, as discussed, is a type of pregnancy that cannot be treated as an intrauterine pregnancy because. . . it's not one. It's dangerous and specific to the location of the pregnancy. Sometimes, the location is unknown, which adds complexity to how it's treated. An ectopic pregnancy is commonly treated using a medication known as *methotrexate*. It's an injection that can be given as early as necessary and may be used throughout the first trimester. Most ectopic pregnancies that qualify for the use of methotrexate are present in a fallopian tube and the tube hasn't yet ruptured, therefore it's not emergent. The closer you get to the end of the first trimester, the more likely the fallopian tube is to rupture.

Sometimes one dose is enough but there are circumstances where two or three doses may be needed. Of course, it's not a fail-proof medication, just like any other treatment plan, so there are times where surgery is needed. The type of procedure depends on the location and size of the pregnancy.

After someone has a dose of the medication, it can take a few weeks for the pregnancy to completely leave the body. Depending on the gestational age of the pregnancy, there may be vaginal bleeding, cramping, and some pain. Some women report having no bleeding or pain, which leads to confusion when we are talking about pregnancy loss.

An ectopic pregnancy is a unique type of pregnancy but it is still pregnancy loss.

SECOND TRIMESTER: SPONTANEOUS LABOR/BIRTH

There is another avenue of birth and loss that I've seen more times than I'd like to admit by being a miscarriage doula, and that is where someone is in the second trimester of their pregnancy and suddenly goes into labor.

There are many examples of women experiencing spontaneous labor at home in the early second trimester. Usually it's between 13–16 weeks and happens very quickly and without much warning. Oftentimes, in hindsight there were signs that were not recognized, which is understandable. It's often caused by their cervix being soft or dilated or a possible infection that caused their cervix to dilate or their water to break.

Black women are more likely to experience this type of pregnancy loss, because they are more likely to have cervical dilation earlier than expected. This is also due to the racial disparity that exists when they seek treatment for things like spotting and cramping. They are more likely to be brushed off for this pain compared to white or Hispanic patients. There's a lot of proof in the history of obstetrics that points to a type of systemic racism that exists, especially in the United States.

Many women who experience a loss in the second trimester are told that it's rare and likely won't happen again. Unfortunately, it's not as rare as you might think. We just don't have access to the appropriate statistics so we don't have a clear understanding of second trimester loss, especially early second trimester loss.

SECOND AND THIRD TRIMESTERS: BEING INDUCED IN THE HOSPITAL

Many women don't relate to the term miscarriage when a loss happens during the second trimester. They might have a medical concern that requires termination for medical reasons or an induction for medical reasons.

When someone is navigating the loss of a pregnancy or child in the second or third trimester, it's often not a textbook case or something that they can easily find resources about. The language that surrounds the pregnancy loss community is either *miscarriage* or *stillbirth*; however, many women don't feel like they fit into either category.

There are people who go to an appointment at 18 weeks and learn that their baby doesn't have a heartbeat. Then they are transferred to the hospital and induced to give birth. Other people might learn devastating news at their anatomy scan and either have to choose to terminate their pregnancy and be induced, or wait and see how long their child lives in utero—still needing to be induced either way. Then there are others who may experience their water breaking at 22 weeks, give birth at the hospital, and either hope that their child lives at that young gestation or say goodbye following birth.

Of course, there's stillbirth and that can happen through a full-term delivery where a baby dies at 39 weeks of pregnancy. It's a shocking, unexpected loss that shakes up the lives of the people going through it.

The bottom line to remember with treatment options related to pregnancy loss is that there are many ways loss can happen and multiple treatment options available. Sometimes we have losses that don't fit into boxes and the care is personalized—it's not a one-size-fits-all experience.

Reflection Prompts

- ◆ Based on the information in this chapter and what was discussed or explained during your own experience with pregnancy loss, what type of pregnancy loss did you experience? Did you understand it when you went through it?
- ◆ What have you learned from this chapter that you wish you knew prior to your pregnancy loss?
- ◆ Language-wise, how do you feel about the term *miscarriage* or *pregnancy loss*? How do you usually speak about your experience?

CHAPTER 3

The Many Layers of Grief

Grief is a complicated aspect of life. Even if you read all of the books, work in a space that deals with grief, and understand it at an expert level, you can't prepare yourself for how you will experience a loss. Throughout our existence, every death, loss of life, or non-death loss feels different, which adds to the complexity of grief.

With that being said, I cannot promise you a blueprint as you walk along the path of grief. I wish that I had all of the answers and could map out exactly how the coming weeks, months, and years will be for you, but it's just not possible. Here's why: it's a unique kind of grief.

One goal I have as a grief and bereavement professional is to make sure that the grief associated with pregnancy loss is widely acknowledged. Sadly, the grief women feel due to losing a child in utero is rarely recognized by those on the outside of that pregnancy. I've heard many times from clients, and experienced it myself, that people are uncomfortable considering a first trimester loss as a death. But then in the second or third trimester, it's also not recognized to the same degree as other deaths are. This creates a stigma around miscarriage.

The emotions of grieving are the part that people can often relate to other people about because we may have similar symptoms of grief even if our types of death are vastly different. People experience grief in many ways and are often seeking community. When the loss experience itself is unique, that's when we start to feel disconnected from the overall grief community.

Pregnancy loss is unique through and through. The reason for its complexity stems from there being so many ways that a death during pregnancy happens, mixed with the differences between the people who experience these losses. It's basically an internal loss that affects us outside of our body but in a way that only we experience and can see.

The Unstable Timeline of Grief

How long will I feel the grief so heavily? This is a question I am asked often. I take a deep breath before answering it because I don't have the magic answer. And I know from the experience of my own losses that people desperately need to be told when things will feel better for them or else it feels hopeless to keep moving through a life that is burdened by sadness and despair.

If I were to give you a short answer to this question, it would be roughly one year from the date of your loss. I recognize that a year feels and sounds like a long period of time when looking toward the future. A year is only short when we are reflecting back on time that has passed. It's an unfair aspect of life—the way time works.

The reason I say a year is because most grieving people, no matter the type of loss they've experienced, feel that the first year after a death is the hardest. You're navigating all of the firsts that you wouldn't have without this loss and there's grief attached to those events. Then you add in the fact that pregnancy loss is unique and there are milestones, events, hopes and dreams, and a life that you are missing. There's a lot of ground to cover in a year. I'm not saying that the grief is magically healed after a year, but it will feel lighter to carry. It's as though you will understand what you need during hard times, which tools feel supportive, and how to communicate your grief with those around you.

I've created a timeline of grief that isn't perfect but it seems to ring true for many of the women I work with (see Figure 3.1). The reason why we don't often have timelines for expected grief is because it's unique to each person. It's important to think of this as the outline for the timeline but there may be days or months from the first-year post-pregnancy loss that feel more difficult or less difficult than expected. Each milestone or hardship that's experienced throughout that first year is a *peak* in grief, which means it feels heavier during that time. But as the peaks and

Figure 3.1 Mapping out a year of events that can be emotionally difficult as you navigate pregnancy loss and the grief that follows.

valleys happen, it's important to remember that the grief gets lighter between the heavy moments.

The starting point for what I refer to as the unstable timeline of grief may feel difficult to pin down if your loss didn't happen on one specific day or if there was a lengthy process in having a diagnosis and/or treatment. In many cases, day one of your timeline is when you learn of your pregnancy loss, whether that's through an ultrasound, blood work, or bleeding. Day one is usually when you feel shocked and numb to the emotions or reality around you. Everyone might connect their day one differently and that's okay. Some examples of day one on the timeline might look like these:

- The day that pregnancy loss was confirmed and the options or plan forward was given

◆ The day of a procedure such as a D&C
◆ The day that bleeding started and the miscarriage began

GRIEF IS NOT A LINEAR PROCESS

Over the weeks that follow your loss, as you physically heal and navigate the emotional process of immediate life after loss, you'll notice that grief will ebb and flow, which is often confusing for grieving people. Having a week straight where you don't want to see anyone or days where you are bedridden with grief followed by a day where you laugh or feel moments of happiness can feel conflicting. If you are not familiar with grief to begin with, then the experience of feeling multiple emotions at once can feel abnormal. The first month is filled with healing, coping, despair, and finding ways to smile again. And then when the calendar shows that you are exactly one month out from day one—you will feel a cloud of sadness on that day because it's often when people realize that their milestones are different now. There's no weekly milestone to celebrate, it's thinking about how long it's been since the worst day.

Followed by the one-month mark of your miscarriage or pregnancy loss is often the first menstrual bleed, and it brings up a lot of emotions. Whether you are someone who conceived without medical intervention or used medical treatment such as IUI or IVF, having a period when you shouldn't be having periods (because you should be pregnant) is a difficult step in the timeline of grief. The majority of the people that I work with feel a mixture of relief and sadness when their first period after pregnancy loss arrives. Again, multiple emotions at once feels confusing. A lot of people think that having a seemingly good and bad emotion at the same time isn't a good sign when navigating grief, but it's actually a very normal grief symptom.

Once someone has a fertility complication, such as an untimely birth and death of a pregnancy or child, they often worry about the future of their fertility. Will they have complications from this miscarriage? Will a D&C (or similar procedure) cause a struggle moving forward? Even though the chances of those things happening are slim, it's natural to worry about the changes that your body will experience after being pregnant in the first place. So, when your period returns and it's on a timeline that your doctor laid out for you—there's a sense of relief because it is proof that your body has healed or is healing. The relief aspect comes from feeling hopeful for the future even if there's fear there, too. Sadness often comes from the realization that your previous pregnancy is fully over and that your body is healing along with you.

When returning to your "normal" or pre-pregnancy lifestyle and routine, you may feel as though you see life differently or have a smaller capacity to take on responsibilities. This is all a normal reaction to grief, and it stems from grief feeling so overwhelming and time consuming that we often struggle to carry anything else. This peak in grief can come in waves because the process of coping with a new normal and re-establishing yourself in your own life doesn't happen at once. You may feel an increase in the gravity of grief and then it settles before something else comes up. This stage of the unstable timeline often includes returning to work if you took time off, socializing with a friend group who might be discussing mundane topics that are difficult for you to connect with right now, attending clubs or hobbies like you did before loss, etc.

TIME TO TRY AGAIN?

The thought of trying to conceive again after loss is yet another stressor point because it can highlight the fear that we have about the future as well as the sadness felt for the child that we've lost and the lost opportunity to raise that specific life. Hoping for another life to enter the world while grieving a life that was lost far too soon or too early in development is complicated to explain to others. We so often hear that family or friends of someone who has experienced pregnancy loss will say something along the lines of at least you know you can get pregnant, you can always try again! As though losing your pregnancy, starting over, and trying to conceive again when you already conceived and experienced loss—can be fixed by getting pregnant again. Oftentimes, getting pregnant again is a huge deal because we are mourning the experience that we once had of being excited and naive. And we should never forget that there are people who cannot have sex and get pregnant seemingly quickly nor does getting pregnant again mean that a child will be born and live a healthy life. There are a lot of uncertainties when it comes to our fertility and future after loss and it's worth recognizing.

DEALING WITH MILESTONES

Different holidays throughout the year will surprise those who have experienced pregnancy loss because we don't often pay them attention in pregnancy unless someone has a due date on a holiday or a significant date. Holidays tend to impact our grieving timeline because they are now a trigger instead of a time where we felt supported or loved, surrounded by friends and family. A few holidays that often take people by surprise (and not in a good way) are Halloween (children and families getting dressed up), Thanksgiving (discussing what you're thankful for during a time where you feel really low), and Mother's and Father's Day (especially if you would like to be acknowledged and aren't). These days can be really painful reminders and it's hard to know ahead of time how you'll react to the holiday itself.

Bypassing weeks or dates that would have been huge milestones are always difficult when navigating that first year after pregnancy loss. These milestones are hard to ignore if you had planned around them when you were in the earlier weeks of pregnancy or if someone in your daily life is pregnant and on a similar timeline as you were. These milestones may be the halfway mark (or the 20th week of pregnancy), gender reveals, baby showers, weekly turnovers, the list goes on. Sometimes it feels like you're living in a parallel universe, especially when you see others on that timeline getting everything that you were planning for.

For those who knew when their estimated due date would be or used pregnancy tracking apps that would tell you an estimated due date based on the start of your last menstrual cycle—this date is engrained in your brain and cannot be erased. It's difficult to navigate because you wish that you could ignore the date itself, but your mind and body will not let you. For others, you may know roughly when you would be due and a select few are unaware of these dates and have an incredible ability to not give in to the pressures of looking on the Internet for specific information. The due date, or estimated day that your baby would have been born on, is a really heavy date for anyone who has experienced pregnancy loss. The buildup and anticipation to the day itself are often the worst part because you're fearful of how you'll feel and you're not sure how to prepare for it. We want to honor our babies without weighing ourselves down with grief, but if we've learned anything during the months prior to that date—grief cannot be controlled or forgotten (even though we may want it to).

And finally—the end of our unstable timeline of grief is the year anniversary of your miscarriage, the death of your child, the birth that was untimely. So much has changed in a year and in some ways, you feel behind where you should be. There's growth mixed with staying still and it can bring up all of the complicated emotions that were experienced during those first few months after loss. The reason why I end this timeline with the year mark is not because the grief ends and at that point. But to make it to this part of the grief process means that you've managed to survive all of the firsts that you would experience throughout pregnancy. Of course, there are always milestones like when they would have started school and so forth, but we already know that grief isn't going anywhere. It's about learning to live alongside grief and not allowing it to knock you down all the time—sometimes is okay but moving forward is the key.

Different Types of Grief

Before experiencing my first miscarriage, I had lost many people in my life. Death came in many forms as I was growing up and then once I entered adulthood, I dealt with the deaths of a few people who were my age and who died by various tragic accidents. I wasn't a stranger to grief and trauma but I also didn't understand that every loss you experience in

life is different. At the time of learning that my first pregnancy was technically a *missed miscarriage*, I thought *I can do this—I've navigated grief
before* but immediately the pain of that loss felt different. The best way
I could explain it was that the grief of losing that pregnancy—that baby—
was internal and personal. Close to my chest.

When it comes to the differences felt in grief that comes with pregnancy or
baby loss, sometimes it's small and can hardly be noticed without careful
attention and then there are times where it feels like the differences have
knocked you down as you've tried to live a normal life after loss.

Here are some types of grief that I see people experience with different
types of pregnancy loss:

+ Normal grief
+ Acute grief
+ Anticipatory grief
+ Disenfranchised grief
+ Cumulative grief
+ Complicated grief

In all honesty, I don't love the term *normal grief* as if there's an abnormal
way to experience grief. There are unhealthy ways to cope with grief but
when it comes to going through a loss, a loss is a loss and the grief that is
experienced is valid and, in a sense, normal. I do think that the word normal means less to us after pregnancy loss though. But saying that someone
is navigating or experiencing normal grief just means they are having common feelings and emotions following a death or major loss (such as the
loss of a pregnancy, the loss of a baby, the loss of a child).

Acute grief sets in immediately following the loss itself, whether it's when
you learn about your miscarriage, start bleeding, or have a procedure. It
encompasses both the emotional response to separation and the body's

reaction to the stress of loss. The emotions that come along with acute grief are often described as overwhelming and difficult to accept—also associated with being in shock. One way that I describe acute grief is that it's like saying "I know that this is happening but it doesn't feel real. I don't know how this has happened."

There are times when someone is experiencing a limbo during their pregnancy and within the days or weeks where they aren't sure of the outcome of their pregnancy, they might start the grieving process with or without realizing it. *Anticipatory grief* is what this is called, and it happens in a lot of cases of pregnancy loss because most losses aren't straightforward and may take a few weeks to fully diagnose. We often hear of this type of loss when someone is terminally ill, and we know that we will have to say goodbye to them soon but aren't sure how much more time there is with them. Of course, pregnancy loss is unique there because we aren't losing someone that we have memories with, know really well, or have photos to hold onto after they are gone. Anticipating the loss of your pregnancy and the loss of a child that you have created dreams for, made plans for holidays, and envisioned what life with them looks like is painful because you don't actually have those clear images or tangible items to cling to the way you would with, for example, a grandfather with terminal cancer.

Disenfranchised grief arises when society denies a person's need, right, role or capacity to grieve. It's a type of grief that is most associated with pregnancy loss because it's a grief that is often not supported or acknowledged by those around us. Another reason why pregnancy loss may be related to disenfranchised grief is that there are social stigmas that naturally invalidate pregnancy loss. One thing that further pushes us to feel disenfranchised grief is when people say things like "at least it happened early" or "you'll get pregnant again—keep trying!" Because it insinuates that the loss wasn't important, maybe that it's not real since it's not tangible, and that the baby is replaceable. All of which are false because the loss of that child is very real and the grief is valid.

Cumulative grief is also referred to as grief overload and people may feel this if they have multiple losses happening at once in life or recurrent pregnancy loss. It can also be seen in people whose losses take longer than expected to occur.

A Theory on the Stages of Grief

Miscarriage and the experience of losing someone who didn't really get to be anyone is a pain that feels so under-recognized that it was difficult to relate to most grief resources. Then I started providing professional support to others through The Miscarriage Doula and learned that most people feel this way. They feel as though their grief is so unique that the resources and support on general grief just didn't fit. The stages of grief being a main point of contention because it led so many grieving people to think that they weren't grieving correctly.

The theory of grief that most people recognize the most is known as the Kubler-Ross Stages of Grief, which was created by Dr. Elisabeth Kübler-Ross and introduced in her book *On Death and Dying* in 1969.[1] Since then, it's been used as a baseline for grief and showcased in film and television to help represent grief.

Dr. Kubler-Ross's five stages are denial, anger, bargaining, depression, and acceptance. Some people find that is very accurate and can relate to those stages. I often hear grieving people express that they were experiencing stages that weren't mentioned in that five-stage layout. It was this realization that made me want to understand the stages of grief and that's when I came across the layout of different perspectives on death and grief from psychologists throughout history and understood it from a deeper level. At the time of my own losses, I couldn't relate to these stages of grief but I sincerely thought that *I* was the problem. It took working in the bereavement space and hearing this complaint from others to validate the suspicion I already had—pregnancy loss is different from other losses.

There are many stages of grief that we could try on to see which fits us best. I've found some that represent pregnancy loss a little better than the Kubler-Ross method. But it's always important to remember that any stages of grief, any timeline on grief (yes, even mine) is just a theory and it's not linear even though we are desperately hoping that we fit the mold. The point is to validate your experience and process your grief.

I discuss relationships and grieving alongside your partner later, but it's important to consider that you and your partner might feel grief and relate to different stages or theories on grief.

> **Challenge for partners:** Sit down with your partner and go over the following theories on the stages of grief. Put 10 minutes on the timer (you can use more if needed) and each of you read over these theoretical concepts of grief. Then sit together and share which you find the most relatable to your version of grief.

With that being said, let's discuss a few other theories on the stages of death.

♦ *Sigmund Freud's Theory of Mourning*[2] is one of the earliest theories on grief and in many ways, it shaped how an entire generation looked at grief. In Freud's model, "Mourning and Melancholia," he suggests that we will stop grieving the dead when we emotionally disconnect from them. Over the years this has been argued because detaching emotionally from grief is not usually a choice someone has, at least to grieve in a healthy and productive way.

♦ *Erich Lindemann's "Grief Work" Theory*[3] was built on Lindemann's research to better understand grief. He started working with survivors of the Cocoanut Grove Fire of 1942, where almost 500 people died in a nightclub fire in Boston. Through his research, he found that there were many symptoms of grief that kept showing in his patients, such as struggling to find meaning in basic activities and tasks, somatic distress (anxiety, fatigue, nausea), seeing mental images of the deceased, and feeling emotions like guilt following their death.

◆ *John Bowlby's Four Stages of Grief*[4] is a theory that's based on attachment, as Bowlby's professional focus was on attachment theory in children and how separation anxiety affects them. He found a connection between attachment and separation and applied them to bereavement and grief. His four stages are shock and numbness, yearning and searching, despair and disorganization, and reorganization and recovery.

There are also a few theories that include action steps to help people navigate grief:

◆ *Therese Rando*[5] is a psychologist who focuses on grief and mourning. She's known for having the belief that grief is more of an involuntary process, whereas mourning is more of an unconscious process, what we do as we continue through life. Rando discusses three phases of mourning—the avoidance phase, the confrontation phase, and the accommodation phase. And within these phases are the six Rs—recognize the loss, react to the separation, recollect and reexperience the deceased, relinquish old attachment, readjust to a new world, and reinvest emotional energy.

◆ *J. William Worden*[6] wrote a theory on navigating grief associated with COVID-19. It's a popular theory that other psychologists use in their bereavement work for other types of losses. Worden's task-based theory is referred to as the "Four Tasks of Mourning": to accept the reality of the loss, process the pain of grief, adjust to the world after loss, and find an appropriate place for the deceased in your emotional life.

There are many more theories on grief, but these are the ones that come up the most for bereavement and moving through life after loss. While the reasons behind each psychologist's research were different (like child attachment theory), I feel like there are pieces of each theory that I can relate to from my own experience with pregnancy loss.

Going back to Erich Lindemann's "Grief Work" Theory, doesn't this sound similar to what we experience in pregnancy loss? There are so many similarities in this theory, especially in the struggling to find meaning in daily tasks, struggling with somatic distress, and seeing mental images of the deceased. I see the last one come up a lot through my work but I've also experienced that distress myself. Seeing the ultrasound where your baby wasn't alive anymore, seeing what they look like when you give birth at home, it all changes how we grieve. From my losses as well as my professional experience supporting people through grief, I find that this theory as well as John Bowlby's theory fits the mold of grieving a child that you don't get the opportunity to raise and watch grow up.

I find that John Bowlby's four stages of grief fit into a particular grief experience that comes with pregnancy loss. The theory is focused on how attachment theory plays a role in grief when a parent loses a child or when a child loses a parent. When a parent loses a child, their grief feels different than losing a grandparent who had a long life. This is the theory that we often follow through the work of The Miscarriage Doula and find that a lot of our clients within the pregnancy loss community feel comforted by these stages. I usually lay out the four stages and list what event during pregnancy loss that fits into which stage of loss, as shown in Figure 3.2.

Any time we look at a theory on the stages of grief, it's important to note that we can lean on whatever feels relevant to our specific grief and that no model is perfect. There may be days, weeks, or months where you feel as though you're between stages; this is normal. You can also jump back and forth between stages because it highlights what a rollercoaster grief is. Honor how you feel. There's no specific blueprint; therefore, it can change as you cope and heal.

JOHN BOWLBY'S FOUR STAGES OF GRIEF

STAGE 1: SHOCK AND NUMBNESS	STAGE 2: YEARNING AND SEARCHING
• The moment(s) where you learn about your loss • Seeing blood/spotting for the first time • Discussing the options for birth/miscarriage with your medical provider • Physical symptoms like insomnia or difficulty breathing from despair	• Question why this happened and wanting to find answers • Purchasing artwork or something in honor of your baby • Fear of trying to conceive again and wanting to have a plan for moving forward
STAGE 3: DESPAIR AND DISORGANIZATION	STAGE 4: REORGANIZATION AND RECOVERY
• Feeling particularly angry or jealous of friend/family members who are currently pregnant and not experiencing loss (even though you obviously wish the best for them—it's still painful) • Struggling with feeling lonely and like those around you don't understand what you're going through • Bitterness within your relationship with your partner (often because they don't have the physical burden of loss and you do) • Struggle to communicate with your partner or feeling like you're not on the same page	• Commonly after your first period following loss and feeling somewhat hopeful that you can and will get pregnant again • Feeling eager to try and conceive again, hoping for a different outcome • Receiving answers from testing and getting a clear plan for moving forward

Figure 3.2   Consider how each stage of grief in John Bowlby's grief module relates to pregnancy loss.

Recognizing Symptoms of Grief

When it comes to pregnancy loss at any gestational age, there are a lot of unwanted emotions or physical sensations that you can experience. Symptoms of grief can be seemingly small or obvious. For some people, it's feeling fatigue and the lack of desire to leave a comfortable space (which is often a home or bed). There is also a chance that you may have increased anxiety, which can show up as heart palpitations, worries, loss of sleep, or a tightness in your chest.

Grief has numerous cognitive effects, including difficulty concentrating, especially for extended periods. This is often referred to as "brain fog," a fitting term because everything feels hazy and mentally exhausting during this time. Cognitive symptoms of grief can manifest in various ways, including vivid, immersive dreams that feel incredibly realistic. These dreams can intensify feelings of grief upon waking, sometimes blurring the line between dream and reality, making it even more challenging to navigate daily life.

Other ways that people feel grief can be through emotions such as sadness, despair, anger, hopelessness, and having conflicted feelings about the future, whether it's concern for your reproductive future or navigating a lack of concern about anything. The emotional element of grief is what is often talked about on a broader scale because these are emotions that most people can relate to.

Did you know that you can physically feel grief? It's a piece of grief that I don't see discussed enough. As a bereavement doula who focuses on pregnancy loss at any gestation, I see many physical symptoms. Women often ask if it's normal to be physically struggling. Some of the physical symptoms of grief include fatigue, phantom pains in the abdominal area, headaches, difficulty sleeping, chest pain or difficulty breathing at times, and soreness in specific muscles (usually arms and legs).

Reflection Prompts

- ◆ Name three symptoms of grief that you experienced during the first month following your pregnancy loss.
- ◆ Based on the types of grief covered in this chapter, what type of grief do you feel has presented itself the most for you?
- ◆ Which theory on the stages of grief do you relate to the most? What stage are you currently in?

Secondary Losses Associated with Pregnancy Loss

Have you ever wondered why the grief from pregnancy loss can feel so incredibly heavy? If so, you're not alone. I often hear from clients who have experienced the death of a parent and believed that was the worst pain imaginable. And at the time, it was. But then they go through a miscarriage at 10 weeks or a second-trimester loss, and suddenly, the depth of this grief feels incomparable to anything they've ever known.

An unexpected aspect of death, especially pregnancy loss-specific deaths, is the long list of unexpected losses we suffer afterward. These are referred to as *secondary losses of grief.* While the list is often unique to the person who is navigating the death, there are a lot of examples of secondary losses.

Sometimes these secondary losses are more obvious as time goes on, while other times they feel like they are piling on at a time where we already feel that grief is too heavy to carry.

Some examples of secondary losses related to pregnancy loss include:

- Loss of the future you imagined
- Loss of identity as a mother in the way you planned
- Loss of trust in your body
- Loss of innocence and naivety in pregnancy
- Loss of control
- Loss of confidence in medical professionals
- Loss of relationships
- Loss of community
- Loss of time
- Loss of a specific date or milestone in your life
- Loss of emotional security
- Loss of intimacy
- Loss of joy in parenting (if you have living children prior to loss)

- Loss of faith or spiritual beliefs
- Loss of workplace support or understanding
- Loss of social events (such as baby showers, weddings while pregnant, and so on)
- Loss of financial stability
- Loss of the ability to enjoy a future pregnancy
- Loss of sense of fairness in life
- Loss of a piece of yourself

A practice that is often useful with my clients is to acknowledge that their grief is multifaceted. Creating a list of your losses can help you name the many different things you are grieving. None of this grief is simple (which I think is a misconception some of us may have prior to experiencing pregnancy loss).

Reflection Prompts

Here are some prompts to help you in identifying secondary losses:

- Aside from the loss of your baby, what other changes, losses, or challenges have you noticed in your life since your loss? Think about relationships, emotions, routines, future plans, or how you see yourself.
- Make a list of all the secondary losses you've experienced. For each one, write a short reflection on what it meant to you and how it has shaped your grief.
- Looking at the secondary losses you've identified, what are some small steps you can take to rebuild or redefine certain aspects of your life? This could mean setting boundaries, creating new traditions, seeking support, or finding new ways to reconnect with yourself.

Check Point: How Are You Doing?

Take the mental health assessment shown in Figure 3.3. Consider how you've struggled with or felt over the last seven days. It is helpful to know which aspects of your pregnancy loss experience you need to focus on, and what to bring to your therapist or medical team.

Over the last week, have you experienced any of the following?

☐ Repeated disturbing memories, thoughts, or images of the pregnancy loss itself

☐ Disturbing dreams of the loss

☐ Flashbacks or intrusive memories of the loss

☐ Strong emotions and crying jags

☐ A trigger (something that gives you physical/emotional response)

☐ Avoiding talking or thinking about your pregnancy or loss

☐ Avoiding any feeling related to your pregnancy or loss

☐ Physical reactions (heart pounding, trouble breathing or sweating) when something reminds you of the loss

☐ Avoiding activities or situations because they remind you of the loss

☐ Having trouble remembering aspects of the physical experience

☐ Distance from friends and family

☐ Emotionally numbed or being unable to have loving feelings for those close to you

☐ Hopefulness about the future

☐ Being misunderstood by your partner

☐ Distance from your partner

Figure 3.3   Mental health assessment.

Seek out support when you need it. If you feel that you need immediate mental health support or believe you are in a crisis, reach out to the following organizations:

- Emergency: 911
- National Domestic Violence Hotline: 1-800-799-7233
- National Suicide Prevention Lifeline: 988
- National Hotline Network: 1-800-SUICIDE (1-800-784-2433)
- Crisis Text Line: Text "DESERVE" to 741-741

CHAPTER 4

Trauma and Pregnancy Loss

Validation is essential after pregnancy loss because the stigma surrounding it can leave women questioning which feelings are valid and which aren't. In my personal experience, I knew that having a miscarriage at home, in the middle of the night, without any preparation, was a life-altering experience. I struggled with showering and using the bathroom for months after my loss, because I would relive the feelings of passing my baby at home. Along with struggling to use the bathroom in my home, I couldn't sleep because I would dream about my miscarriage or see flashes of images as I tried to fall asleep. For so long I wrote this off because one thing I knew about myself was that I was a sensitive person. Things affected me more than they seemed to affect those around me. Therefore, I considered all of this an overreaction.

Following my second miscarriage, which happened four months after the first one, I saw my therapist and opened up about my struggle with personal hygiene and sleeping. As someone who has obsessive-compulsive disorder (OCD), I knew that I couldn't keep the symptoms to myself any longer because they didn't feel *normal* in any sense of the word. It was at this appointment that I learned I was struggling with Post-traumatic stress disorder (PTSD) and it was clear that it was disrupting my life.

My first instinct was to deny that I could have something like PTSD because I did not view myself as a warrior, a soldier, or a survivor. While this diagnosis sounded intimidating to me, it also felt like I didn't earn that badge. My therapist then told me that trauma comes in many forms and sometimes we don't realize that an event is traumatic until it affects our life afterwards. In many ways, that appointment was validating but also very overwhelming.

I had never deemed a miscarriage as traumatic, although if someone had told me that they went through a miscarriage and were traumatized, I would completely validate that experience. From the outside, it would sound traumatic. But when it comes to myself, I leaned into negative self-talk instead. All of which I've now learned so many women struggle with post-pregnancy loss, and the education on trauma or the validation of one's experience is often difficult to find.

There's a reason we seek out resources and support after a death or traumatic event: our minds are often flooded with conflicting emotions, the world suddenly feels unfamiliar, and we're left trying to understand why everything hurts so much. It's understandable to have questions about grief and it's common to question if the life-altering event you just experienced was traumatic or not. The hard part is that only you can determine those answers.

What Is Trauma?

Trauma is a psychological response to an event that overwhelms a person's ability to cope, often involving fear, helplessness, or a sense of danger. Psychologists Camille B. Wortman and Jessica A. Latack say that

"A death is considered traumatic if it occurs without warning; if it is untimely; if it involves violence; if there is damage to the loved one's body; if it was caused by a perpetrator with intent to harm; if the survivor regards the death as preventable; if the survivor believes that the loved one suffered; or if the survivor regards the death, or manner of death, as unfair and unjust. Other deaths typically regarded as traumatic include those in which the survivor witnessed the death; those in which the mourner is confronted with multiple deaths; and those in which the survivor's own life is threatened."[1]

Their definition of trauma is an incredible validation of reproductive trauma because there are terms that we often use following a traumatic event such as "preventable," "unfair," and "unjust." I also find that the word "untimely" fits pregnancy loss perfectly because it's literally an untimely birth, a birth that occurred prematurely.

Separate from trauma, grief is an emotional response that we have when either someone dies or we experience the loss of something we once had, or should have. The truth is, we can grieve almost anything that vanishes from our lives whether it's a person, a relationship, an event, or an inanimate object that we've misplaced or lost.

While grief doesn't often involve physical pain, it can cause a sense of danger. Trauma often contains a threat, and whether it's to someone's physical well-being or emotional state, the emotional control is often affected. With pregnancy loss, our brain often feels as though it's in a crisis, especially as you recover from the experience itself. It can feel like you're *stuck* in a traumatic situation because escaping the fear or crisis-mode isn't necessarily easy for the traumatized person but with therapy and somatic-centered healing, it is possible.

An aspect of trauma that is particularly difficult is that it often comes with grief. It's a two-for-one deal that no one wants any part of but, sadly, life is filled with it. In cases outside of pregnancy loss, a lot of people have experience with trauma, and it can be due to a traumatic death of a loved one or it may be a non-death loss. For example, when someone has a traumatic childhood that has left them with some battle wounds of trauma as they enter adulthood—their grief might revolve around the fact that their childhood experience will never be what they deserved or what they witnessed others have. They are grieving the childhood that they didn't get to have. But with pregnancy loss, you are traumatized both by the experience, and by grieving your pregnancy, or your baby.

So, the correlation between the two seems separate by definition but when we look at real-world examples, it's obvious that trauma and grief often go hand in hand.

All the Ways that Pregnancy Loss Can Be Traumatic

Many women ask if pregnancy loss can be a traumatic event and the answer is deeply personal and based on many factors. Not every death is seen as traumatic and there are different layers to trauma just as there are to grief. What I've found in the online pregnancy loss community is that those who feel that they are traumatized from their loss experience don't feel validated in expressing that trauma. Women who do not feel traumatized feel guilty because they fear that others will think that means they aren't grieving properly. You can see how it's a no-win situation. The community might feel divided, confused, or like they need more validation before processing the potential trauma experienced.

Multiple studies have shown that both women and their partners can experience significant psychological effects as early as one month after a pregnancy loss—including symptoms of anxiety, depression, and post-traumatic stress disorder (PTSD). In a 2022 study conducted through three Early Pregnancy Units in central London, participants completed email-based questionnaires using the Hospital Anxiety and Depression Scale (HADS) and the Post-Traumatic Stress Diagnostic Scale (PDS). The results revealed that individuals with a prior mental health diagnosis were more likely to meet clinical criteria for anxiety, depression, or PTSD following a loss. Those who had experienced previous losses were also at higher risk. Notably, the study found that women often had poor insight into their own mental health prognosis—leading researchers to conclude that all individuals who experience pregnancy loss should be considered at risk for psychological distress, regardless of their history.[2]

An earlier study performed in 2016 found that a large number of women who had early pregnancy loss or an ectopic pregnancy fulfilled the criteria for PTSD for up to three months following the loss itself.[3] Working with many women who have suffered ectopic pregnancies, I see what their experience does to their mental well-being, especially as they are hopeful to become pregnant again. There is a specific distrust in your body that can cause a paranoia in early pregnancy or until you rule out the possibility of another ectopic pregnancy.

There is sufficient data that validates the trauma that women experience during pregnancy and pregnancy loss. With this information, our society could better understand the pregnant person's experience of carrying a pregnancy, losing that pregnancy, and navigating life after loss.

As someone who experienced miscarriage over six years ago and now works full-time with people who are navigating pregnancy loss in real time and dealing with the aftermath of this loss, I can clearly see how pregnancy loss is traumatic. However, I also remember what it felt like to be freshly postpartum after loss, which we will discuss more of, and afraid to admit that my experience of giving birth on my toilet was traumatic. Doesn't it sound silly to question if that is traumatic?

There are a multitude of ways that miscarriage and pregnancy loss at any gestation can be traumatic:

- ◆ Without even considering the types of pregnancy loss that occur, the physical aspect of miscarriage or birth in the first, second, or third trimester when your baby isn't alive is a really difficult thing to experience.
- ◆ Having a miscarriage at home is often seen as traumatic because of the level of blood loss, the decisions that have to be made, and seeing what the pregnancy looks like once birth happens.
- ◆ Having a medical procedure such as a D&C or D&E can cause a lot of medical trauma for various reasons.
- ◆ Second or third trimester birth with a fatal outcome is difficult because people are either in labor prematurely and admitted to the hospital, or they are admitted to the hospital and then induced.

Every angle of pregnancy and neonatal loss feels impossible.

Let's look at some examples based on the different types of pregnancy loss and the trauma that often happens alongside them. These are not listed in any specific order.

- *Chemical pregnancy:* One element of what's referred to as a chemical pregnancy that is often traumatizing is the fact that women don't have validation from their support people or medical team. This is especially true when the miscarriage aspect happens within the same day or few days following a pregnancy test showing a positive result, when many women feel that their feelings are minimized by others. The emotions that come with this type of loss are often conflicting for the person going through the miscarriage, which might lead to medical trauma.
- *Blighted ovum:* While this falls under the missed miscarriage umbrella, I always like to acknowledge this type of loss because it comes with a lot of medical trauma for people who experience it. Often, it seems that the language used when diagnosing this type of loss is what sticks with the person going through it—referring to the amniotic sac as *empty* is a very confusing statement seeing as the person is pregnant.
- *Missed miscarriage:* The trauma that comes with experiencing a missed miscarriage is often a mixture of medical trauma and the trauma of not feeling connected to your body. When you're pregnant, you get the feeling that you and your body are one. Then when you find out that you've been pregnant with a baby that stopped growing weeks prior, you start to question that connection and feel like you can't trust the body that you live in.
- *Second trimester loss (at home):* When someone gives birth in the second trimester and it happens at home, it's often not expected and happens spontaneously. These types of loss typically occur between 13–16 weeks but due to different circumstances can happen at any

time. In my experience as a bereavement doula, these women do not know that it's happening until their water breaks and labor begins, which is a traumatic experience for various reasons: the shock value, the bleeding, the pain, and not knowing what to do (plus calling an ambulance or going to the hospital is also traumatic).

◆ *Second trimester loss (at the hospital):* Induction does occur when someone experiences the death of their child in the second trimester. While most women that I speak with have a decent hospital experience (meaning the nurses and staff were supportive and helpful), the experience of giving birth to a child prematurely and not alive, is traumatic at baseline. From seeing your baby, holding them, creating memories that they are only physically a part of—it's devastating.

◆ *Termination for medical reasons (also known as TFMR):* Most people can understand why any type of pregnancy loss is traumatic and with TFMR, the trauma is turned up a notch because there are a number of steps involved, and a lot of the medical side of a termination is traumatic. From making the compassionate decision to have a termination due to medical reasons, to scheduling, preparing, and going in for the termination itself, then the birth element—there's no *easy* part of this process. Emotions that often accompany the trauma of TFMR are guilt and shame.

◆ *Stillbirth:* While the definition of stillbirth often covers pregnancy loss after 20 weeks, I feel that most people feel confusion around what type of loss they have experienced. Many people who reach the *viability stage* of pregnancy (which is somewhere between 22–24 weeks gestation) feel they relate more to term stillbirth because their baby could have (potentially) survived outside the womb. In these cases, women learn that their baby no longer has a heartbeat and this could happen through 42 weeks of pregnancy, prior to birth occurring. Just like other losses, learning about your baby not having a heartbeat is often a traumatic experience. With stillbirth specifically, women can often remember the last time they felt their baby kick, which adds a lot of shock and confusion to the mix. Giving birth to a baby that should still be alive and that should be able to live outside of your body is a traumatic experience from many different perspectives.

The physical experience of birth, whether it's at home unmedicated, in a medical setting, or expected or not, is often traumatic for people who are going through pregnancy loss. Trauma isn't reserved only for the woman—partners may also experience trauma from pregnancy loss. The forms of trauma for them might be more focused on their loved one's life or being concerned about their experience, yet they do show signs of trauma following pregnancy loss.

Trauma Responses You May Experience

There are many times where someone is struggling with the trauma of their pregnancy loss experience and doesn't realize that the symptoms they are fighting on a regular basis are actually trauma responses. We already know that each person is different and the way they react to trauma will also vary from person to person. However, some of the trauma responses may look alike, which is what helps us relate to others and seek professional help. It's also important to mention that both the birthing person and their partner can be traumatized from a miscarriage or pregnancy loss at any gestation. Trauma may show up differently in a partner who didn't experience the physical element of trauma but it exists nonetheless.

Some responses to trauma may look like these:

- *Emotional responses:* Feeling panic, rage, numbness, or being unable to regulate emotions
- *Physical responses:* Trouble sleeping (whether falling asleep or staying asleep), hypervigilance or increased anxiety, somatic symptoms (such as pain, headaches, dizziness), flashbacks

- *Cognitive responses:* Intrusive (unwanted) thoughts, dissociation, trouble retaining memories
- *Behavioral responses:* Avoidance, isolation, compulsive behaviors

For the partner, the trauma responses follow the same list but focus on different areas. I my experience, partners often struggle with avoidance, isolation, trouble sleeping, and dissociation. There is a lack of support for the pregnant people navigating loss and even less support for their loved ones. Stigmas follow us everywhere we go and they exist for our loved ones as well. Regardless of the gender of the partner, the most common comment I hear is that partners seem as though they are "over it" when it comes to grief and loss.

In my experience, I realized that my husband was showing some signs of recovering from a traumatic event. Since I didn't seek support until after our second missed miscarriage, I didn't recognize the pattern or symptoms until after the fact. Our first miscarriage happened in the middle of the night, at our home, and he was present for every horrible moment of it. I realized that my miscarriage was happening when I woke up with the urge to go to the bathroom. I had to walk across the house to the bathroom and luckily, for whatever reason, that night I brought my phone with me. When I saw the amount of blood and realized what was happening, I called his phone and he came running within seconds. After that night, I realized that every time I woke up and got out of bed earlier than usual, he would sit up with a panicked expression and say, "Is everything okay?" Looking back, I feel remorseful because I was annoyed by this. I did not put the pieces of the puzzle together.

My husband's brain held on to the trauma of that miscarriage and when he felt my body shift the bed, even though he was asleep, his brain was on high alert and he would wake up to make sure there wasn't something bad happening. This eased after a few months. My symptoms were often more severe, including panic attacks, intrusive thoughts, and insomnia. However, his trauma was important and I wish I had known then what I know now—our partners can be traumatized from navigating pregnancy loss just as we are.

Reflection Prompts

- ◆ What moments from your loss do you find yourself replaying the most (if any)?
- ◆ In what ways has your body felt different (physically, emotionally, or spiritually) since the loss?
- ◆ What does the word "trauma" mean to you and does it feel like an accurate description of your experience?

CHAPTER 5

Dealing with the Triggers of Loss

Anytime we experience a death, a loss, a traumatic event, it's basically inevitable to experience triggers, too. In a society where people use the term "triggered" out of context, it can be difficult to know if you're triggered, what being triggered means, how long it can last, and what to do about it. We often don't realize how often the term is misused until we are in a situation where we are experiencing triggers, feel triggered, and then feel shame over being in a heightened state of emotion.

I've been a part of many support group discussions that revolved around triggers that we anticipated after pregnancy loss or baby loss and then experiencing a random trigger that we weren't prepared for. It's a harsh reality of dealing with triggers and it proves that we have no control over how our brain will react after a loss. But I don't know anyone who regrets over-preparing for a trigger, so understanding what's happening in your brain and what actions you can take is the first step to navigating through these landmines.

What's a Trigger?

Unfortunately, a trigger can be literally anything that we interact with or come across on any given day. More specifically, a trigger can be a smell, taste, sound, memory, or a certain location that can bring back memories or thoughts about a life-changing, traumatic, or difficult event (such as a miscarriage, giving birth prematurely, or losing a child). That trigger then creates an emotional, and often physical, response.

Just as there are layers to grief, there are also many layers to being triggered, feeling triggered, and interacting with something that is a trigger for you. You can plan for or anticipate some triggers, while others may catch you by surprise. There's no "good" way to feel triggered and even if you can't prevent it or control your response, preparing for the worst-case scenario is helpful.

COMMON TRIGGERS FOLLOWING PREGNANCY LOSS

The list of examples is long, and triggers are specific to you and your experience with pregnancy loss. However, these are some common triggers:

- Seeing a pregnancy announcement
- Finding out someone close to you is pregnant and due on a similar timeline
- Returning to the doctor's office or hospital where you received bad news or experienced your loss (often the waiting room and the exam room are particularly painful)
- Seeing baby or ultrasound photos (social media, from friends or family)
- The smell of prenatal vitamins (or their existence in your space)
- Certain songs, seasons, or even foods you associated with being pregnant
- Being asked, "Do you have kids?" or questions about your fertility and family size

Before working in the grief space and studying what grief and trauma can do to our body and mind, I was the victim of pregnancy loss and desperately needed this type of information. As someone with previous traumas, I expected to move on after pregnancy loss. Instead, I added another traumatic event under my belt. One of my general symptoms of coping tended to be avoidance, which I do not recommend, and when my first missed miscarriage occurred, I thought that I could ignore the trauma. Sadly, that isn't how it works.

I had triggers that many people in the pregnancy loss community can relate to, such as feeling heart palpitations when I see a pregnancy announcement on social media, feeling numb when seeing ultrasound images of healthy babies, and dates or milestones that I was missing. But there were a few instances that took me by surprise, and I feel that they highlight the severity of someone being triggered after a traumatic death or loss.

The first time I experienced an unexpected trigger was a little over a month after my first miscarriage. My husband and I went to eat at a local Tex-Mex restaurant. During my pregnancy, I craved shrimp fajitas, eating them far more often than I would care to admit. A month after that miscarriage, we decided to go out to dinner to take a break from the grief. I was feeling more inclined to stay home and be alone, so this was an attempt to get outside of the house. I ordered something other than shrimp fajitas because I wasn't craving them anymore. It didn't occur to me that this could be a trigger until I heard the sizzle of fajitas being brought out from the kitchen going to another table. My eyes filled with tears and at first, I didn't know what was happening other than I was now randomly crying at the dinner table in a public place. It wasn't until talking through it with my husband that I realized that for a moment I thought that a sizzling plate of fajitas was coming to our table. My brain held on to the memory of going out to eat while I was pregnant and enjoying faji-tas more than any other time. Now I was no longer pregnant, and the reminder was upsetting. The symptoms I felt were heart palpations, crying, and a bit of panic in the moment. From that experience, I was able to anticipate it for the next time we went out to eat, however, that was a one-time type of trigger.

Another trigger that in one way or another comes up for many people who have experienced pregnancy loss is exposure to blood. For some it's their monthly menstrual cycle and the bleeding may remind them of their miscar-riage or that they are no longer pregnant. Others who struggle with trauma from pregnancy loss might experience intense symptoms to blood as a trig-ger, such as flashbacks, disassociation, avoidance (especially of rooms such as the bathroom), and so forth. This trigger affected me the most—seeing blood and the physical sensation of bleeding. As a woman, vaginal discharge is a normal part of my menstrual cycle, and it's also a big part of pregnancies that occur after loss. The feeling of increased discharge was very triggering for me because it mirrored the feeling of passing tissue during each of my miscar-riages. Periods were also difficult for a mix of reasons. For one, seeing blood was difficult because I could feel my body go into a fight-or-flight response and what helped me was saying "I am safe" over and over again as I changed my sanitary napkins and tried to leave the bathroom as swiftly as possible.

But then there are painful periods and, sadly, I have those along with heavy bleeding during almost every menstrual bleed. The feeling of blood clots and seeing heavy bleeding for multiple days was incredibly difficult.

While these examples of triggers are just a small portion of what can be disruptive to a grieving person's experience after loss, it's important to sit with yourself and ask yourself if there are any triggers you anticipate. How can you prepare yourself so you can anticipate your reaction?

COPING WITH A TRIGGER (IN THE MOMENT)

When you are triggered, it's important to lean on tools that assist in calming your nervous system. It's important to keep an open mind as you navigate through life after pregnancy loss because you never know what will be difficult and what won't be as difficult. There's no rulebook and while that's frustrating to hear, it's also the truth.

Imagine that you're in a public place and you feel triggered. Maybe a pregnant woman who looks to be about as far along as you *should* walks by. Your eyes immediately fill with tears, your chest becomes tight, and an emotional reaction overcomes you. Without putting thought into this situation beforehand, you freeze up, panic, and don't know how to comfort yourself.

Having good coping tools can make you feel safer and more prepared, even if it's helpful in the smallest way possible.

Here are some common tools that are recommended by therapists and mental health professionals:

- ◆ Pause to breathe deeply while placing your hand on your chest or belly and remind yourself that you're safe. It can also be helpful to say, "I'm safe" (out loud or as a thought).
- ◆ Try the "5-4-3-2-1" technique, which is naming five things you can see, four you can touch, three you can hear, two you can smell, and

one you can taste. I know that the last thing you *want* to do in a moment where you're struggling is to think through this sequence but it helps calm your nervous system so that you can approach the moment and work through it.

◆ I often work with clients on creating a "disaster" plan for moments they know will be hard. Some things that you might put on this plan are a support person you can call or text when you're feeling down or triggered, reminders that it's okay to skip events that are difficult emotionally, and grounding techniques that are useful and helpful to you.

Always remember that this is a season and like everything else, grief will ebb and flow, changing as time passes. There may be some events that you expect to be difficult, but then they end up being fine, without a single trigger. It can be helpful to be prepared but always keep in mind that you can't predict which triggers will be heavy and which will be easier to manage. It's okay to feel whatever feelings surface.

You can't force yourself to *move on* so instead continue to provide support for yourself as you navigate forward, carrying grief with you. In the next chapter, I break down coping with the grief of pregnancy loss.

Setting Boundaries Surrounding Triggers

One important point to understand about triggers is that they don't follow a timeline. This means they can continue to affect you long after the initial loss. You may encounter difficult moments when you're struggling the most, even while surrounded by others. At times, you might need to decline invitations or avoid certain gatherings to protect your emotional well-being. Because of this, it's important to communicate openly and set boundaries that honor your grief.

After pregnancy loss, boundaries are a crucial part of protecting your emotional well-being and mental health. Here are some reasons why boundaries may be necessary after loss:

- There may be people in your life who make insensitive comments or ask personal questions, both of which you're uncomfortable with. Setting boundaries can help eliminate the risk of this person causing you harm.
- Grief is exhausting and not everyone understands that. Some people might try to "fix" the problem, which only leads to more pain.
- To avoid triggers altogether, it's helpful to set boundaries with individuals or groups of people as you navigate landmines of triggers and are trying to take care of yourself.
- You may want to keep details of your fertility journey private. Even if you've shared some details with a select few people, you can always pull back on how much you share. Some people use boundaries as a way of preserving their autonomy.

Setting boundaries isn't as simple as it sounds. It's hard to say, "I don't like that" and expect someone to respect you, apologize, and never say it again. To set boundaries, you have to put a lot of care and attention into it. There might be times when you have to repeat the boundary over and over again.

When setting boundaries, make sure you are clear and straight to the point. The people may push back or disagree and that's okay. Your peace is worth the effort. If someone doesn't respect your boundaries, you can limit your exposure to them or avoid sharing information with them.

It's important to remember that we are all humans and we make mistakes. It's possible for someone to forget about a boundary and unintentionally break it—that's when you might need to remind them about the boundary.

Consider these scripts for setting boundaries with people:

♦ "Thank you for the invitation. I'm not in a place right now where I can attend events like this, but I appreciate your thinking of me."

♦ "That's a really personal part of my life, and I'm not ready to talk about it. I hope you understand."

♦ "I know you mean well, but I'm not looking for advice right now. I'm just trying to get through each day."

♦ "Can we talk about something else? I need a break from everything related to pregnancy and loss right now."

Reflection Prompts

♦ Name a trigger that you've identified prior to reading this book. What is it? What emotions or physical sensations came up when you came in contact with that trigger?

♦ Do you feel that your pregnancy loss experience was traumatic? If so, in what ways was it a traumatic experience for you?

♦ What's a coping strategy that has helped you in the past? If nothing comes to mind, what's a strategy that you'd like to implement in the future?

CHAPTER 6

Coping with the Grief and Reality of Loss

Grief after pregnancy loss isn't something that we experience in a straight line. It doesn't follow the rules, and it doesn't care what kind of day we're trying to have. Some mornings, you might feel like you can breathe again, and by the afternoon, you're completely undone by a song, a smell, or an unexpected thought. That's the reality of loss. It rewrites how we move through the world and how we interact with people.

Pregnancy loss, especially in a world that often ignores it, can feel incredibly isolating. You might find yourself asking, "Why is this still affecting me?" or "Why can't I just move on?" But here's the truth: grief isn't something to get over. It's something to carry, and learning how to carry it—in a way that honors your experience and allows you to keep going—is the work of coping. It's exactly the premise of moving forward, not moving on.

In this chapter, I don't talk about *moving on* because, as you know, we don't move on from this loss. I discuss what holding your grief as you navigate the world can look like, what it means to actively cope with the loss of your child, and what moving through the world looks like for the bereaved. Remember, there's no one-size-fits-all path here. There's just your path—and it's valid, no matter what it looks like.

What Does It Mean to Cope with Loss?

Most people associate coping with how they're doing emotionally on any given day. If someone has a day where they're triggered multiple times, cry at least once, or feel the weight of their grief more than usual, I often hear them say, "I'm not coping well." And every time, it breaks my heart.

It breaks my heart because I've been there—stuck in the same misconceptions. Every belief about what it "should" look like to cope, I've held at one point or another. Especially in the early days of loss. It doesn't help that the grief of pregnancy loss is already so isolating, stigmatized, and rarely talked about. It's easy to assume we're doing it wrong when no one tells us what it can actually look like.

Grieving is hard enough as it is. There's no map to follow. But when it comes to pregnancy loss—a grief that's often invisible to the outside world—finding any kind of validation in the aftermath can feel impossible. That lack of visibility makes so many people feel like they aren't coping, or aren't coping well enough.

> The truth is, coping and grieving are deeply personal. There's no one-size-fits-all definition. They look different for everyone.

To really understand coping, we have to talk about what it means. We all have experience with it—whether it's grief from death, or the weight of a life-altering event like a global pandemic, political injustice, or personal betrayal. Sometimes coping looks like comfort. Sometimes it looks like a distraction. Sometimes it looks like doing absolutely nothing. On the surface, it sounds simple: do what helps you feel grounded, safe, or okay—even for a moment. But in reality, it can feel like one more thing you have to figure out while surviving something you never asked to go through.

In the context of pregnancy loss, I define coping as any action—big or small—that helps you reengage with life after loss, or simply brings you a little comfort in the midst of it. There's no timeline. No right way. Just trial and error and a whole lot of grace.

Coping Styles: What's Yours?

There are many factors to determining what type of coping tools will be most effective for you as you navigate through grief and any trauma that you've experienced throughout the process of your specific loss (or losses). For starters, your personality and the things you enjoy about life outside of grief play a role in how you support yourself during a difficult time. For example, if you're an introverted person, then attending an in-person support group might not be helpful for you at first (or at all).

It's important to remember that what works for one person may not work for you and that doesn't mean you're *coping incorrectly*. Lean into the things that are helpful for you, try new tools or activities and don't be afraid to say *I didn't find that helpful so I won't do that again.*

Just like the different theories on the stages of grief that people experience, there are also a lot of styles or types of coping strategies and again, a lot of what you feel compelled to try or do falls back on your personality and what's helped you in the past.

UNDERSTANDING THE COPING STYLES

From a grief counseling point of view, there are four categories of coping that are often used in therapy-like settings:

- *Problem-focused coping* is based on the organizational side of grief. You crave information and seek validation (which can help the distress that a lack of control causes). This type of coping is utilized by people who are planners or participants in active coping. You might search for the *why* and need to have answers before considering another pregnancy or before being able to fully process and move through your grief.
- *Emotion-focused coping* reduces the negative emotions that are associated with grief, in this case pregnancy loss. Some would look at the name of this type of coping and assume it had more to do with sensitivity, crying, and showing emotion (which are all totally okay to do by the way), but this approach focuses on finding positive reframing, acceptance, or forgiveness (to yourself and others), or turning to religion or some sort of spirituality belief.
- *Meaning-focused coping* is when the bereaved uses cognitive strategies to find peace in grief or meaning in their loss. This happens in many different ways but includes mindfulness, journaling, and discussing your loss and being a resource for others.
- *Social coping,* also called support-seeking, is the type of coping that I often see because people come to me to help them grieve.

This type of coping involves seeking and leaning on support from community. Whether it's friends, family, peer-led support groups, or professional support groups, seeking community support is a huge asset to many grieving people.

It's important to remember that there's no right or wrong here—there are simply different methods because human beings are unique.

Another way to explore what coping might look like for *you* is by asking a simple question: *When I've gone through something difficult in life, how have I responded?* Do you tend to process things emotionally, rationally, or creatively? I like this approach to coping styles because it builds on things you probably already know about yourself. Instead of starting from scratch, it invites you to pay attention to how you naturally move through hard things—the habits, tools, or outlets that have helped you feel better in the past.

Examples of emotional coping, rational coping, and creative coping may look like these:

♦ People who lean on creative coping strategies find that writing, creating art, participating in a hobby, or listening to music are helpful as they navigate through grief after pregnancy loss. There are many different things you can do to find a creative outlet for your grief.

♦ Rational coping involves finding information or tools to understand loss. You might use that information to silence any guilt or shame that you feel. These type of grievers are also good at organizing and planning.

♦ People who cope emotionally lean into their emotions and own the feelings that come up in grief. A good cry is something they lean on after a difficult day. Or they journal and create space for the emotions instead of avoiding them.

There are healthy and unhealthy ways to cope. When you're focusing on coping in a healthy way, you are processing your grief so it can eventually feel lighter to carry—remember that grief doesn't just vanish.

I find that women often compare their progress to others, especially in a group setting. Even if one woman has more bad days than good days (or vice versa), neither woman is doing a better job at coping than the other. At the end of the day, it's about surviving and doing so in a way that makes your life better in the long run. Whether that means being able to go out in public without breaking into tears, telling your story on a podcast, or journaling consistently, it is up to you.

HEALTHY VERSUS UNHEALTHY COPING

You may be more aware of negative coping than you are with positive or healthy coping strategies. Following my first miscarriage I remember thinking to myself that I shouldn't have a glass of wine because I didn't want to enjoy the way that disassociation felt in case I leaned into it further. We often have preconceived notions about what's a good way to cope and what's labeled as bad. In reality, the glass of wine is more so a problem if the drinking becomes excessive or constant.

Women who have suffered a miscarriage often want to have a glass of wine (or some sort of alcoholic drink) in a rebellious action because they *shouldn't* be able to have that drink. So, I see clients having one or two drinks following their loss and oftentimes they are in tears as they do so because they don't want this drink—they want their baby. If you find yourself relating to this section, take a moment to go easy on yourself, because grief is difficult and no one can prepare you for the reality of this experience.

Healthy coping can look like this:

◆ Getting outside (sitting, standing, or walking) and taking in fresh air when you're feeling triggered by grief.

- Leaning on something that has been helpful to you in the past, such as a hobby, a sport, attending a show or concert, or anything else that you find fun.
- Arranging for you, a partner, a friend, your family, to go on vacation and temporarily escape the stressors of everyday life while grieving. Sometimes going to a new location, with people you love, can help.
- Believe it or not, crying is a healthy way to cope, even though it might not feel good while you're actively crying. The relief after is something that is considered to be a *good* thing. A healthy cry can include sharing your story with a friend and having space to cry, watching a movie where you relate to a character regarding your grief and you cry, or journaling—writing to your baby—and crying.
- Joining a support group and finding community in others who have suffered from pregnancy loss.

Unhealthy coping can look like this:

- Isolating yourself regularly. This is different than skipping on an event or social gathering that may be triggering. Avoiding friends, family, or the general public can lead to more isolation. While this is a common way to feel, especially directly after pregnancy loss, isolating yourself can lead to further grief.
- Being in denial that your baby is dead, that you aren't pregnant, and avoiding the reality of the situation you're in.
- Taking more risks that could cost you your life, or feeling like you don't value your life to the same level you did before.
- Disassociating and shutting down emotionally when you have strong emotions. The truth is, grief is uncomfortable and no one wants to feel the pain. For many of us, suppressing them is a natural urge.
- Drinking excessively or using substances.

A question that comes up often for my clients is whether avoidance is okay or damaging. The truth is, avoidance is a confusing element of coping because it can actually fall into both categories: healthy and unhealthy.

Avoiding something (or someone) temporarily while you ready yourself to reenter the world is okay. It's when we avoid doing something (like paying our medical bills) or avoid seeing someone without communication (like a pregnant friend) that it starts to become harmful.

The truth is, the emotions that we experience while coping with grief or trauma are complex. We have the ability to feel multiple emotions at one time. Our capacity for emotions is far greater than we realize until we are in a position where we feel overwhelmed by them.

If you've found yourself leaning on some actions that are deemed negative in the world of grief and coping, know that is okay and it's normal. There's time to work your way through grief in a way that's meaningful to your life. Shame and guilt are such a huge aspect of grief following pregnancy loss and it often feels impossible to find relief from the burden of those emotions. When you're leaning on things to help you cope and then see them on a list of things that are *negative*, I know firsthand how that doesn't help the shame that you already feel. Remember that you are doing the best you can and it's likely that you picked up this book in seek of support, which *is* a positive form of coping. Don't be too hard on yourself—you are navigating something that often feels unbearable.

Reflection Prompts

- ◆ What have you noticed about the way you've been coping since your loss—what feels supportive and what feels heavy or harmful?
- ◆ When your grief feels overwhelming, what are three small actions you can take to ground yourself or soothe your body?
- ◆ What role does avoidance play in your coping?

CHAPTER 7

Your Relationships After Pregnancy Loss

Relationships shape our lives—whether we're actively seeking them out or not. From romantic partners and parents to grandparents, extended family, close friends, coworkers, and even those more surface-level connections—like the person you chat with every Tuesday at your workout class or during school pickup—we're constantly coming into contact with others. And it's not just face-to-face; virtual interactions count too. The way people respond to us during difficult moments reveals a lot. It often becomes a painful but powerful lesson in who truly shows up and who we need to create some distance from.

What's interesting is that we each hold different relationships close for different reasons. What feels sacred to one person might feel casual to another—and that contrast can be eye-opening, especially when life gets hard.

Women who experience pregnancy loss are not a monolith. They come from all walks of life—heterosexual couples, same-sex partners, single-mothers-by-choice, those surrounded by a strong support system, and those walking this path alone with quiet courage. Grief doesn't discriminate, and neither does the need for understanding, care, and connection.

In this chapter, I explore how the relationships in our lives can deeply impact the grieving process—sometimes offering strength and comfort, and other times compounding the hurt. I take a closer look at how these connections shape healing and influence the way you move forward after loss. Depending on where you are and what type of relationship you're navigating and maybe even struggling with, the goal of this section is for you to take what you need.

On Romantic Relationships

This section is for those with a romantic partner (life partner, spouse, or significant other).

Women who experience pregnancy loss within a romantic relationship—whether it's a marriage, a long-term partnership, or even a relationship that developed quickly and/or unexpectedly—often find themselves falling into one of two categories. Either they feel closer to their partner or they feel a disconnect from the person they love and care for and wonder if something is wrong with the relationship. Pregnancy loss affects our relationships in many ways and those effects change over time because our grief shifts and changes as we move forward through life.

Research shows that couples who are married or living together face a higher risk of relationship strain or separation after a miscarriage—and that risk increases even more after a stillbirth.[1] A 2010 study set out to look deeply into marriage and cohabitation outcomes after pregnancy and found that in the United States, just 57% of first marriages and 31% of first live-in partnerships last at least 15 years.[2] Following miscarriage, fetal death, or child loss, the marital dissolution rates rapidly increased over 15 years compared to the control group of people who have living children and no pregnancy or infant loss. The authors of that study saw an increase in relationship and marital dissolutions between six to eight months following pregnancy loss.

As someone who has experienced loss and a hardship in my relationship due to the disconnect of our grief, I find this information to be incredibly validating. And I know that it's something clients often bring up in support sessions or a group setting. We are told that it's not appropriate to discuss such personal issues or the details of a personal struggle but the truth is that if we discuss it, then we may realize that we aren't alone and that is often worth the risk.

One of my clients—I call her Sammy—once shared how isolated she felt in her grief because her husband just didn't seem to *get* what she was going through. They had lost the same child, so why was he such a stranger to this grief? In the early days, her husband was visibly heartbroken.

He mourned the daughter they'd never get to meet, hold, or know, especially after pathology confirmed the baby was a girl. He recognized that the loss was real and painful. But as time went on, Sammy found herself struggling in ways he couldn't fully understand. She avoided baby showers because they were too triggering. She wept quietly in the bathroom each time her period arrived—grieving the daughter she missed *and* the fact that another month had passed without a new pregnancy. For Sammy, the grief lived in her body and followed her through everyday moments. But her husband, trying to be supportive in his own way, encouraged her to focus on the future and "stay hopeful." His response, though well-intentioned, left her feeling unseen. The emotional gap between them became undeniable—a painful reminder of how differently a couple can experience the same loss.

Just like anything else, there's a range of support that we can receive from a partner. I've also met partners, both male and female, who felt the grief as deeply as their pregnant partner. As a bereavement doula, I've come to learn that there are a lot of factors determining how much a partner relates to such intense emotions. This revolves around personality and emotional intelligence mixed with how they are known to handle hardships in other places of life.

A common misconception I often hear is that having a female partner somehow makes grieving easier—because, generally speaking, women are perceived as being more emotionally open or more willing to express their grief outwardly. Being someone who has supported and witnessed the grief of many same-sex couples, I often see that the female non-pregnant partner is more supportive of emotional support, such as their loved one doing therapy. They are also more supportive and understanding of the fact that grief takes time and there's no point where someone should be *over* a miscarriage. I believe that to be partly because they can empathize with the biological needs that come into play after losing a baby or how a menstrual period can be triggering and upsetting. These are things that male partners cannot understand to the same degree.

When it feels like there's a disconnect between you and your partner, someone you love and who has been there for you during other difficulties, it is important to make sure you're taking time to communicate. When it comes to therapy or grief coaching, you'll hear this recommendation a lot. This is more than saying, "Hi honey, how was your day?" Communicating with your partner through grief includes more emotional work than you would normally do because you each need space to talk while also actively listening and hearing what the other has to say.

Here are some of the tips that I share with my clients:

- Write down how you're feeling (and be honest) and then use what you've written down to guide a conversation with your partner. Or you can let them read what you've written. This can help you feel more prepared for a difficult conversation while also giving them the ability to process your words and feelings. You can also give them your written feelings and say, "Let's sit down together in a half hour to check in with each other and discuss managing this grief."
- Remember that while you've lost the same pregnancy and the same baby, you might experience grief differently. Try giving space to your partner to share their reflections on the physical loss.
- Schedule routine check-ins with your partner. Some couples call this an HR meeting, a household meeting, or a family check-in—whatever works best for you, go with it. Don't let anyone tell you that it's abnormal to schedule time with your partner to discuss things such as struggles or grief; sometimes knowing *when* you will have the time to discuss it in depth helps organize your thoughts and feelings.

Reflection Prompts

Prompts for reflecting on grieving with your partner: These prompts are great for journaling and checking in on how you're feeling with your partner and their support during this time.

♦ How has grief shown up in your relationship or communication with your partner?

♦ Have there been moments when it felt hard to connect or understand each other since the loss?

♦ Has your experience with loss or infertility affected physical or emotional intimacy with your partner? In what ways?

♦ What feels different or tender when it comes to intimacy now, if anything?

♦ How do you and your partner tend to cope differently with grief? Has that created any tension or understanding between you?

Prompts to discuss grief and pregnancy loss with your partner: These prompts invite you to have a deeper conversation as a couple, check in on how each other is doing, and find ways to support one another.

♦ What has been the hardest part of this experience for you?

♦ How has this loss affected how you feel connected to me emotionally and physically in our daily lives?

♦ What's something you wish I knew or understood better about how you're grieving?

♦ Have your hopes, fears, or views about the future changed? What feels comforting or overwhelming to think about together?

♦ What can we do—or say—to stay connected even when we're grieving differently?

♦ Are there things we've avoided talking about? What feels hard to say out loud?

For Single Mothers by Choice

This section is for women who navigate a fertility journey using sperm donation with the intention to be a single parent through pregnancy, birth, and raising the child.

The road to parenthood can be complicated. There are quite a few ways to become a mom or dad and sometimes people do it on their own. While men can also be a single parent by choice, for the sake of the theme surrounding this book, I talk about the women who embark on becoming a mother without a romantic partner (or without a partner who will be involved with raising the child).

In case you don't know, SMBC (single mom by choice) is when a female seeks out a sperm donor and tries to (or successfully) achieves a pregnancy using ART (Assisted Reproduction Technology). Some women look at a sperm donor database, choose the sperm, pay for a specific amount, and then work with a fertility clinic through IUI or IVF to get pregnant. Other women may have a male friend or close acquaintance who is willing to donate sperm at no cost, unlike purchasing from a sperm bank. An IUI (intrauterine insemination) is when the sperm is placed directly inside the uterine cavity around the time of ovulation. With IVF (in vitro fertilization), a woman's eggs are carefully retrieved from her ovaries after she takes medications designed to stimulate and accelerate their growth. The eggs are then fertilized with sperm—using donor sperm in this example—with the option to perform genetic testing before freezing the embryos or proceeding with a transfer at a time thoughtfully chosen by the woman and her doctor.

When someone goes down this path, it can create some tension in romantic relationships because it's not exactly a walk in the park to tell someone you start dating that you're undergoing fertility treatment and hope to be pregnant in the near future. Or to meet someone while you're pregnant.

Jackie, a client of mine, came to me after a miscarriage that she had as a result of IVF as a single woman. She was 39 at the time and said that she had always wanted to have children and be a mom. Jackie worked in a male-dominated field and it was incredibly important to her to be taken seriously and to work her way to the position she desired. She achieved that goal but the cost, in her eyes, was that she didn't get the chance to really date and fall in love. A year before we met, when she was 38 years old, she went to a fertility clinic and started the process of buying donor sperm and doing IUIs, which led to negative pregnancy tests, so she moved to IVF. She became pregnant and was ecstatic—this was everything she wanted. She felt like living proof that you could have it all and on your own terms. Sadly, at 10 weeks pregnant, she learned that her baby no longer had a heartbeat and she had to have a D&C procedure.

She navigated through her miscarriage, and the entire fertility process really, alone, and she was okay with that. It's what she signed up for after all. But she didn't expect to have a miscarriage and she didn't know that going through a miscarriage and being the only person who knew and loved her child would hurt so bad.

While dating after her miscarriage, she felt disconnected from connecting with other humans and didn't know how to talk about herself without talking about her experiences at the fertility clinic or the baby she'd held in her body for 10 short weeks. I met with her shortly after her miscarriage and she expressed to me that because she had been pregnant, she deleted dating apps and wasn't seeking someone to spend her life with. But now that she'd had a miscarriage and didn't know when—or if—she wanted to try and conceive again, she wanted companionship. But she felt confused on how to discuss the choice to do this alone.

People who enter into this *journey*—which never feels like a word that covers the vast experience of navigating the fertility space—don't always experience loss and when it all goes *according to plan*, then they are prepared because they knew what they were signing up for. Working a miscarriage or any type of pregnancy loss into the arrangement doesn't often come to mind (because who would want to think about miscarriage) so the lack of support becomes painfully obvious.

So how do you cope? Your marital status doesn't change the grief you feel for that baby, but it can change the way you feel about the process and the world. When women who don't have a romantic partner join our support groups, and they hear about other women in the group having supportive partners, it's uncomfortable because their experience is different. While sperm was used to make that baby, the pregnant women didn't know that donor and cannot grieve the loss of their DNA that created a baby. This a complicated aspect of grieving as a single parent and even though it's a choice—that doesn't make it a simple one.

For Those No Longer with Their Partner After Pregnancy Loss

Human relationships have many layers, which makes it difficult to fit this section into a single box. It's true that most of the people I meet with are married or in a long-term relationship and decided *I'd be okay if we got pregnant* and don't use protection. Then there are people who are in relationships and aren't necessarily desiring a pregnancy, using protection and all, and still get pregnant. I think it happens far more than we realize.

This section talks about grieving the loss of a pregnancy, a baby, and a relationship. I call this compounded grief or cumulative grief. When someone has multiple losses happening at the same time, it's difficult for the brain to keep up and it often feels like they can't handle the amount of pressure the grief creates because they don't know what to process first.

Most of the clients I've worked with who are no longer with the partner describe the breakup or dissolution of the relationship as especially painful. There's often a feeling of a permanent biological bond—the deep and undeniable reality that they created life together—even if the pregnancy didn't continue. The grief is not often about the partner but the link they now share with each other and how there won't be another chance for a baby that shares the same biological makeup as the one that was lost. There's profound grief in that and the emotions that follow often surround this life that could have been.

While coping with the pregnancy loss is covered in Chapter 5, there may be some additions to the tools used to grieve the collection of losses that have occurred. Using coping tools for each loss—the pregnancy/baby and the relationship—is wise. This can be journaling and having separate spaces for each loss.

On Family Dynamics

Not everyone understands the difficult nature of grieving the loss of a pregnancy and a child.

After a pregnancy loss, many people notice significant shifts in their relationships with family members. Sometimes, parents of the grieving person say the wrong thing, however well-intentioned. An uncle might unknowingly ask when a baby will be welcomed into the family. Grandparents often don't have much of a filter when it comes to personal matters.

Every family looks different. Some families are supportive and compassionate, while others are distant, critical, or uncomfortable with grief. There are many people who don't have a large family network, or who aren't in contact with their family at all. Some families are separated by distance, some relationships have faded with time, and others have become estranged due to deeper wounds.

The thing that I hear the most about family dynamics is that people don't react to the news of pregnancy loss as the grieving person expected.

We share the vulnerable news with the people who care about us with the hope that there will only be supportive words and kind gestures, but the truth is that a lot of people don't know how to react to grief.

Death, by society's design, is uncomfortable, which doesn't make much sense seeing as everyone will have to navigate death occurring around them at some point in their life. It's often the extended family that will say one of the "at least" statements that don't serve us well. Such as *at least you know you can get pregnant,* or *at least it happened early,* or when someone has their miscarriage at home (which is often a traumatic experience) and someone says *at least your body knows what to do.* None of those statements are helpful. These people often have good intentions, it just doesn't always translate properly.

One aspect of grief that comes up in various topics throughout this book is secondary losses. The losses that we experience because of our main loss. This includes financial loss, identity loss, the loss of an experience, the loss of a role, and so on. When it comes to family members, sometimes we grieve for our loved ones and the role they would have played in the baby's life. For example, if you were pregnant with what would have been your parents' first grandchild—you may grieve that role for them and carry that grief yourself. It's not fair to do that to yourself but it is a part of grief that is for a lack of better words, uncontrollable. You are who you are and you feel what you feel—coping with that is what's important. Such as reminding yourself that this loss happened *to* you and you did not maliciously take away your parents' ability to be that baby's grandparents. As sad as you feel for them, you should feel for yourself (honestly, a little more for yourself).

Another aspect of grief is when to set boundaries and who to set boundaries with—usually it's someone in the family. Do you want people to visit with you? Would you like your space? Would a meal train be helpful? Should you delegate one person to tell others? And so forth. It's okay to keep to yourself for a while after pregnancy loss and it's okay to decline support from one person and take the offer from someone else. Whether your family is close or not, it can be a lot to manage visits with family members, phone calls, FaceTimes, and other communications.

If you have a family member who says a hurtful comment or isn't helpful to your healing after pregnancy loss, don't be afraid to use phrases like these:

- "That's not helpful for me right now."
- "I appreciate you wanting to check in. Right now, I'm not ready to talk about the pregnancy or what's next."
- "I know you mean well, but I'm finding it hard to answer questions about the future right now. Thanks for understanding."
- "It would help me most if you just listened, without trying to fix anything."
- "This is a really sensitive time for me, and I need to ask that we avoid talking about babies, pregnancies, or family planning for now."

On Friendships

Found family is a term used to describe when a friend is so intertwined in your life that they are practically family. You can lean on them, you can trust them, and they have your back when you need them. People often find more support from friendships than they do with their respective family members and that often surprises the grieving people that I personally speak with. Along with finding a great amount of support, friendships are put to the test by hardships, such as when navigating pregnancy loss, grief, trauma, and a shift in their identity. It's a lot for the person going through it and it takes kind, supportive people to truly be a friend during trying times.

While some friendships are the lifeline in our grief, others may be an added stressor or an unexpected trigger that we now have to navigate. Friendships suffer because of pregnancy loss, which is an aspect of loss that we aren't prepared for. Whether it's because priorities change, communication isn't as great as it was before, or a friend becomes a trigger (often if a friend is pregnant), navigating these relationships is challenging.

It's possible to maintain friendships throughout your fertility journey and for some relationships, it's simple. We may learn who we can count on and who we should keep at a distance. There will be times where we learn that a friendship isn't where we thought it was, which requires even more grief to be added to our plate.

Maintaining friendships after pregnancy loss often requires intentional, honest conversations. If you have a friend you want to remain close to, it can help to talk openly about sensitive situations—for example, how you'd like to handle future pregnancy announcements. Would you prefer that they text you instead of telling you in person? Would they understand if you need to step back for a while to protect your own heart?

Communication can ease a lot of tension, but it's important to recognize that not everyone is open to these kinds of conversations, and that's okay too. If your friend does become pregnant, it's possible to still attend gatherings or spend time together, as long as you allow yourself space to feel your emotions—even if that means crying afterward. Being around pregnant friends may bring up complicated feelings, including the bittersweet ache of "happy for you, sad for me."

Some friends may not know the right things to say, or they may unintentionally cause pain. In these moments, don't be afraid to gently guide the conversation by saying something like, "That's not a helpful thing to say right now," or by expressing what you need more clearly. And if a friend repeatedly shows you that they aren't someone you can lean on, it's okay to create distance and lean more heavily on the people who are able to meet you where you are. Grief can reshape our friendships, but it can also reveal the relationships that are strong enough to grow with us.

As you move through grief, you may start to notice which friendships feel safe and which ones leave you feeling more isolated or misunderstood. Safe friendships tend to feel steady, even when words aren't perfect—you feel seen, heard, and respected in your grief. These friends don't rush your healing, don't pressure you to "move on," and are willing to meet you where you are emotionally, even if that changes day to day.

Unsafe friendships, on the other hand, might leave you feeling dismissed, judged, or even blamed for your emotions. You might notice yourself dreading conversations or feeling emotionally drained afterward. It's okay to honor what you feel and to recognize that it's not your responsibility to maintain connections that add more hurt to your already heavy heart. Setting boundaries, limiting contact, or even stepping away from certain friendships isn't selfish—it's a necessary part of protecting your healing space.

What does a supportive friend look like?

◆ Someone who listens without judgment and isn't afraid to sit in silence with you (meaning they don't try to fix what you've gone through or give unsolicited advice).
◆ Someone who checks in multiple times following your pregnancy loss, remembers dates, appointments, and doesn't take it personally if you don't answer their texts quickly.
◆ Someone who understands that grief can make every task more difficult and doesn't put pressure on you to tell them what you need them to do, they just offer to do things for you (such as bring by dinner, help with child care of living children, assist with getting rid of baby items, and so on).

- ◆ Someone who is validating and never follows up something you say with a story about themselves (unless you ask for them to share relative stories and information).

What does an unsupportive friend look like?

- ◆ Someone who doesn't check in with you more than once or doesn't acknowledge the great loss that you've experienced when they do speak with you.
- ◆ Someone who takes the needed space from social situations personally and gets upset with you over it.
- ◆ Someone who puts pressure on you to be healed and moving "on" (which as we know, doesn't actually happen).

Consider these example scripts for setting boundaries with friends:

- ◆ "I'm taking some space to heal, and I'll reach out when I feel ready for more conversations."
- ◆ "I'm grieving, and I'm realizing that certain topics are just too painful to talk about right now. I hope you can respect that."
- ◆ "Checking in with a simple 'thinking of you' text means a lot right now, even if I don't always reply."

On Acquaintances and the General Public

Reentering the world after pregnancy loss is multifaceted.

The world looks different after you've experienced a traumatic loss. It impacts you every day and it might feel like no one except you understands. Women who experience the loss of a pregnancy might feel foggy or like reality doesn't seem real. Some say that this is denial and for some, it is. Being happy and pregnant one day and devastated the next is difficult to process. For women who had a troublesome pregnancy the entire time, the constant anxiety of the shoe finally dropping is heavy to carry for days or weeks on end.

A majority of my clients report feeling nervous about social gatherings. It's for a variety of reasons, usually surrounding having small talk with others, the risk of being asked a personal question such as, "When are you going to have a baby/When are you going to have another baby," and not feeling completely like themselves to the point that they are uncomfortable in public.

Grieving people often struggle with returning to work, attending baby showers, weddings, holiday gatherings, or even just going out in public. It can feel like all eyes are on you, even if that's not the case.

It's important to remember that you deserve time off from your social life, especially where you are struggling and in need of support and care. It's not unreasonable to expect people to understand, but you also don't have to share the personal details with anyone.

Building Your Village

Grief can feel isolating, but you don't have walk through it alone. Even if your circle is small, having people who truly *see* you can make all the difference.

This activity is about identifying the people—or even just one person— who can be part of your village as you navigate life after loss.

Take a deep breath and think about your connections. Trust your instincts.

- ◆ Who feels safe enough to handle the raw, unfiltered version of you?
- ◆ Who listens without trying to fix you or rush you forward?

- Who can sit with your silence without getting uncomfortable?
- Who shows up not just for you, but also for your partner (if you have one)?
- Who has *already* shown up for you, even in small ways—a text, a meal, a memory shared?

If your list feels shorter than you hoped, that's okay. It's not a reflection of you—it's a reflection of how the world sometimes struggles to meet grief where it is. You are allowed to guard your energy. You are allowed to out-grow people who can't meet you where you are. Remember that you can find connections through therapy and support groups.

CHAPTER 8

Dealing with Recurrent Pregnancy Loss

Four months after my first miscarriage, I learned that I was pregnant again with the help of ovulation-induction medications, a protocol laid out by my fertility clinic. I knew that having back-to-back miscarriages was a possibility, but I clung to the fact that I was a healthy, 25-year-old woman with regular cycles and no underlying health conditions. Looking back, I see that version of myself as naive because even being all of those things won't guarantee someone a full-term pregnancy.

At the first ultrasound of my second pregnancy, we were told that it was likely another miscarriage because the embryo didn't develop and was behind in growth. While my first miscarriage was blindsiding and heartbreaking, learning that my second pregnancy held the same fate made me feel numb.

How would I survive another miscarriage? What if every pregnancy we conceive ends like this? What's wrong with my body? These were the thoughts running through my mind. I couldn't make sense of how we were here, again.

The emotional weight of experiencing two or more losses during pregnancy feels all-consuming because it's difficult to ignore the thoughts that something is wrong. Even though recurrent pregnancy loss happens fairly often, statistically, it's less likely to happen, which only adds to the magnitude of the experience.

Through my work as a miscarriage and pregnancy loss doula, I've met women who have suffered two, three, four, even seven losses, and not everyone knows the options that exist following two miscarriages. This chapter discusses recurrent pregnancy loss in depth and answers questions that you may have but haven't voiced yet.

Defining Recurrent Pregnancy Loss (RPL)

The definition of recurrent pregnancy loss in terms of medical testing and care may depend on what country you live in. Medically speaking, when someone experiences multiple pregnancies that end in pregnancy loss for whatever reason, the term used is *recurrent* but you may also see the word *reoccurring*—or you may not know which word to use when speaking about your experience in general. By definition, reoccurring means that something has happened again but doesn't specify how many times it's happened. *Recurrent* also doesn't specify how many times something has happened but refers more to a pattern, which is why so many people believe an RPL diagnosis to require more than two losses. For this reason, some doctors say that women don't have any options medically until they suffer three back-to-back losses.

In the United States, the definition matters because it's how women can get insurance coverage for their healthcare needs as it pertains to recurrent pregnancy loss. There are two organizations that set the tone for these definitions, treatment protocols, and so forth.

One is the American College of Obstetricians and Gynecologists (ACOG), which publishes and supports doctors of Obstetrics and Gynecology (OB-GYNs). It defines RPL as two or more pregnancy losses and recommends a collection of physical exams and blood tests.

The second organization is the American Society for Reproductive Medicine (ASRM), and it creates the guidelines for care from fertility care specialists such as Reproductive Endocrinologists (REI)—also referred to as fertility doctors and clinics. ASRM defines recurrent pregnancy loss as two or more losses as well.

Before 2012, their recommendation was testing after three losses, which is why some doctors will still recommend testing following three losses. In the last 10 years, we've seen an increase in acknowledgment following two pregnancy losses and more preventative measures taken to ensure someone doesn't have an underlying reason for multiple losses.

Causes of Recurrent Pregnancy Loss

Some people may notice a pattern with their pregnancy losses. Maybe they happen at the same gestational period, or they have spotting that occurs in the first trimester of every pregnancy. However, there's not always a pattern and it's often difficult to get to the root of the problem either way. The truth is, women's health and reproductive health are terribly understudied and underfunded, which leads to a lot of unknowns. When we seek fertility testing, we are often following guidelines from our medical team. There are many reasons why loss can happen, especially multiple times, but the testing to confirm these reason may not always be available.

Here are two examples of women who have recurrent losses.

Sam's first pregnancy resulted in her living daughter who is now four years old. She and her partner decided that they were ready to conceive another child. A few months into trying to conceive a second child, Sam had a positive pregnancy test and celebrated the news of a new pregnancy without any concern regarding a miscarriage. Two days after her positive pregnancy test, she started to bleed and was concerned for her pregnancy, so she went to urgent care where they did blood work and confirmed that her HCG levels were too low and that she was likely having a chemical pregnancy. Sam grieved this loss and tried to conceive again right away. Four cycles later, she was pregnant again, now for the third time. She was hesitant to share until after she had an ultrasound due to what happened during her second pregnancy. The first ultrasound was at seven weeks pregnant, and she saw a heartbeat and was measuring right on track due to her last menstrual period. She and her partner took this good news and decided to announce their pregnancy to their daughter and extended family members. When they went back for another ultrasound at 10 weeks along, they learned that, unfortunately, Sam was

(continued)

experiencing a missed miscarriage and her pregnancy stopped growing between 8 and 9 weeks of pregnancy. She now had experienced two miscarriages and qualified for seeing a fertility specialist or seeking blood work to find a reason why her losses happened; however, she's reminded that each of her losses could have been for different reasons since there's no pattern to her losses.

Laura does not have living children and has been trying to conceive for over a year. Throughout the year of trying to conceive, she's suffered three missed miscarriages. They all happened in a similar pattern. Each of her first ultrasounds are at seven weeks' gestation. At that appointment, she learns that her pregnancy is measuring two weeks behind. At five weeks, there's no cardiac activity. She's told to come back in one week to check for growth or progress and when she goes in for the follow-up ultrasound, there's no growth and a miscarriage is confirmed. With each miscarriage she's had a D&C. After the second and third pregnancies, they did pathology testing to learn if there was a genetic reason for her losses. Laura knows that at least two of the three pregnancies were "normal" in terms of trisomy diagnoses and doesn't have a clear answer for her losses. However, the pattern tells her doctor that something specific is going on, and her doctor recommends some additional testing to search for a reason why her losses may be occurring.

There are three major categories of recurrent pregnancy loss:

◆ **Genetic reasons or concerns.** Some miscarriages result from a random genetic factor, while others are due to a couple being diagnosed with a genetic abnormality that may cause pregnancy loss.

◆ **Anatomic abnormalities.** This can include uterine septum, bicornuate uterus, or other uterus shapes that cause pregnancy complications. Intrauterine adhesions can be a concern following birth of any kind or trauma to the uterus. Fibroids and polyps are also common reasons for an anatomic concern, but they are often treatable.

◆ **An array of other medical concerns.** This ranges from hormone imbalances, thyroid disease, diabetes, abnormalities of the immune system, and blood-clotting issues (thrombophilia).

But of course, those are vague categories and usually how medical providers will categorize a reason for a miscarriage or pregnancy loss. Let's really dig deep into the causes of pregnancy loss so that you can better understand what you need to advocate for and what might be happening within your body.

◆ If you've had multiple early losses then it could be a result of the uterine lining being too thin (too thick could be bad too but we often see too thin being more of a concern), which means your estrogen is lower than it should be at the beginning of your cycle. If your estrogen levels are too low, they can be treated using medications, creams, and patches.

◆ Following ovulation (or an embryo transfer or IUI), your progesterone should be over a specific level (higher is better when it comes to progesterone). If your progesterone is too low it can impact your egg quality and the "stickiness" of your uterus, which is important for a successful implantation. Some people with low progesterone may have early losses or ectopic pregnancies. Even losses that happen at 8–10 weeks can be caused by low progesterone. Progesterone, as it pertains to pregnancy, should be tested by blood work and can be treated by a prescription of intra-muscular injection, vaginal suppositories, or oral medication.

◆ Low ovarian reserve is another reason that pregnancy loss occurs. Testing your ovarian reserve can determine the number of eggs you have for your age and if the amount is considered within a normal range. Ovarian reserve can help us understand things like egg quantity, egg quality (or help us theorize on this), as well as confirm if someone is ovulating each cycle or not. The Anti-Müllerian Hormone (AMH) level can be tested by blood at your primary care provider, OB/GYN, or fertility clinic.

◆ A concern that most fertility specialists have, especially if all testing has come back normal, revolves around egg quality. The only way for us to understand a woman's follicle or egg quality is by looking at the egg itself and tracking the process when an egg fertilizes and grows to be an embryo. IVF helps confirm when egg quality is too low but not everyone can do IVF (or has the means to). If someone has low egg quality it could cause infertility, early losses, or multiple losses, especially with chromosomal abnormalities.

◆ Blood clotting, even beyond different disorders, can be a cause for pregnancy loss at any gestational age of the pregnancy. The fact that as humans we can have blood clots that are both fatal or not is a commonly overlooked fact. People can have a blood clotting disorder—medically referred to as thrombophilia—or they could have blood clots that affect blood supply in pregnancy. We know that in pregnancy a woman's blood volume doubles or triples, which means there is a strain on our heart to pump all of this blood, and that can lead to blood clots. It's a topic that remains understudied but is recognized widely by fertility specialists.

◆ Other anatomic concerns include presence of scar tissue, whether from a previous birth, a surgery, or from trauma to the uterus (or cervix). This concern comes up often with recurrent pregnancy loss due to the fact that there's been obvious trauma to the body whether through having a miscarriage at home or procedures such as a D&C. It's also possible that tissue has remained from previous pregnancies and wasn't identified. When looking at all possibilities for loss, this is always something to double-check.

◆ Diseases such as endometriosis, endometritis, and adenomyosis can lead to scar tissue and make fertility and pregnancy very difficult. Just like many other things, they are under-researched, which is why we often have to advocate for this care. A few options for diagnosis and treatment are ultrasounds, tests such as ReceptivaDX, or exploratory laparoscopy to search for endometriosis. The treatment for these diseases would be surgical removal but may be cared for during fertility treatments if removal is not possible or recommended.

- Autoimmune disorders are a large cause of recurrent pregnancy loss and infertility and can be found by blood work in most cases. These can cause issues with egg quality, uterine lining, and during pregnancy itself.
- The cervix plays a large role in pregnancy. Early cervical opening—called incompetent cervix, but I don't like that terminology—seems like an issue relegated to the second trimester only, but, in fact, cervical issues can be a cause of loss as early as 10 weeks of pregnancy. They may be caused by anatomic issues or something like bacteria or infection.

This is not a complete list, but it shows that there are many reasons why loss can happen. We often have a hindsight bias that makes us feel as though we could have done something to prevent our losses and without the information that we often have after the fact, we can't do much to help a pregnancy during a miscarriage or loss in any trimester.

The Emotional and Psychological Impact

Just as I've discussed grief and trauma in general, there's an added layer when someone suffers multiple pregnancy losses. To have one loss is horrible, devastating, and feels unjustified—all of which is a valid way to feel because it is a terrible thing to navigate through. There's something about a second, third, or fourth loss that breaks your spirit and hope moving forward and that's hard to repair. I fear that a common misconception about recurrent losses is that people aren't as pained by the second, third, or fourth, but that's not true at all. Each loss carries its own grief, trauma, and despair. Instead of carrying the weight of one loss, there are multiple losses to carry and then secondary losses for each, such as dates, milestones, timelines.

In my own experience with back-to-back missed miscarriages, I immediately felt broken following the second miscarriage. The fragility of life was almost too much to think about and I couldn't even consider trying to conceive again because the thought of that number going up and up made me feel defeated.

During my first pregnancy, a close friend of mine was pregnant and three weeks ahead of me. When that loss happened, I knew that I would watch her go through her pregnancy and while I was over the moon for her, I was also sad for me. Then four months later, when she was over halfway through her pregnancy, I was pregnant again and I was so hopeful that the second pregnancy would fix everything. Her baby shower was the day after I would have been nine weeks pregnant and I made sure to schedule my ultrasounds so I would know if I had good news or bad news—that way I could decide how to handle her baby shower (which she gave me permission to miss or back out of at the last minute). The day before her baby shower, I learned that my second pregnancy was also a missed miscarriage. How could this happen *again?* She was understanding that I wouldn't be in the emotional headspace to attend her celebration, but she also knew how much I loved and cared for her.

What many people don't realize about miscarriage in general is the toll it takes on every aspect of your life. Then with added factors such as infertility or recurrent miscarriages, it starts to feel like you are the girl who cried pregnancy and you fear that people will stop feeling hopeful for you when you become pregnant.

NAVIGATING THE MEDICAL SYSTEM

When it comes to seeking medical care following recurrent pregnancy losses or during months on end without achieving pregnancy, there can be confusion, misunderstandings, and differences in care depending on where you live. The complexity of the care may lead people to avoid seeking it out or cause additional stress at a time already filled with grief and fear.

In the United States, the guidelines that are provided by the American Society for Reproductive Medicine (ASRM) and the American College of

Obstetricians and Gynecologists (ACOG) determine the current protocol for fertility testing. It's recommended that initial blood panels and tests be performed after two clinically acknowledged pregnancy losses. If someone is under the care of an OB/GYN, they may ask for a referral to a fertility specialist. However, referrals aren't always necessary.

The next step, following a second loss, is to make a consultation appointment with a fertility specialist—formally called a reproductive endocrinologist. These doctors go through medical school, an OB/GYN residency, and then a residency in Reproductive Endocrinology and Infertility (REI). I often refer to them as the specialists prior to pregnancy and during the first trimester, while an OB/GYN specializes more in second trimester, third trimester, birth, and pelvic health. To find the right fertility specialist, you may want to search Google, ask friends who have navigated the fertility space, or visit sites such as Fertility IQ and Resolve, which focuses on fertility care and advocacy.

ADVOCATING FOR YOUR HEALTH

It's important to stand your ground and communicate your concerns with your doctor. In my more than four years of experience supporting people through this process and season of life, I've learned that advocating might sometimes mean that you have to feel uncomfortable, which naturally doesn't feel right. While it's important to trust your doctor and have doctors that you can trust, you also know your body the best and deserve to have your concerns addressed.

Helpful language when advocating for yourself may look like this:

- ◆ "I'm uncomfortable getting pregnant again without further testing and without addressing these concerns."
- ◆ "Seeing a fertility specialist (and/or getting fertility testing on me and my partner) will help me feel safer in my next pregnancy."
- ◆ "Recurrent pregnancy loss is not a normal occurrence nor is it bad luck, so there must be a reason for these losses or something that

can be done to support me in my next pregnancy. I insist that we do testing to look for blood clotting disorders, hormone imbalances, and other factors that could involve my uterus and my partner."

FERTILITY TESTS FOR RECURRENT PREGNANCY LOSS

Even after experiencing one miscarriage, you may want to discuss testing options with your doctor. If you start to see a fertility specialist, these tests are often run following a second pregnancy loss but could also be requested if you wish to do more testing. These are tests that are often performed to search for a cause of recurrent pregnancy loss, and they may be referred to as the *recurrent pregnancy loss panel*. Some doctors may use that name but may not include all of these tests so it's always good to understand the tests that way you can advocate for more, if needed.

Of course, these are not all of the tests available in the world, but they are a starting point for fertility testing. You can always add others as they come up in discussion or become available. For current testing recommendations, always double-check the ASRM website. It's also important to note that these tests should be done after your first period returns following a miscarriage and after your HCG levels are back down to zero. Some tests may require a follow-up or recheck.

Testing in the Recurrent Pregnancy Loss Panel

The following are standard hormone tests found in an RPL panel:

- ◆ Thyroid panel: Having undiagnosed thyroid disease or an unbalance in thyroid hormone levels can lead to infertility or pregnancy loss. The thyroid is a key player in reproductive health and it's important to have a full thyroid panel. These tests are thyroid antibodies (TPO), TSH, T4, Free T4. (These tests can be completed at any time and may need to be repeated periodically, especially once pregnant or when HCG goes to zero.)

- Anti-Müllerian Hormone (AMH)/Ovarian Reserve: Testing ovarian reserve gives women a good idea regarding the number of eggs they have based on their age. It's important to note that this test doesn't give an idea of egg quality, nor can it give a direct number of eggs that someone has in their ovaries. (This test can be completed at any time.)

- Progesterone: A crucial hormone to healthy menstrual cycles, conception, and pregnancy is one that is often under-tested and can lead to many concerns in pregnancy. Progesterone is released from your ovaries and is necessary to have a healthy uterine lining that assists in implantation but also keeping the embryo and early fetus healthy while waiting for the placenta to take over production of nutrients and hormones. When testing progesterone, it's important to test on specific days and in intervals where you can compare the results. Prior to pregnancy being confirmed, you should test 7–10 days following ovulation and it's best to test for three days in a row to make sure your progesterone levels don't lower too early in the cycle. During a pregnancy, you can test your progesterone as soon as you get a positive pregnancy test. The level in pregnancy should be over 20 with a level that falls in the range of 10–19 meaning you should re-test or take prescription supplemental progesterone. A level under 10 in pregnancy often indicates a miscarriage but fast attention may or may not change the outcome of the pregnancy. (Blood tests should be performed on days 7–10 following ovulation or after a positive pregnancy test and repeated once more.)

- Estrogen: A hormone that is important for having healthy menstruation and to support a healthy uterine lining prior to pregnancy. When estrogen is tested, it's often during the first week of someone's menstrual cycle. If someone has early losses or chemical pregnancies, they may want to check their estrogen and uterine lining. This can be treated by adding estrogen to the protocol. (A blood test should be performed on day 3–5 of a menstrual cycle.)

(continued)

Here are some other tests in the panel that can be completed at any time:

- Vitamin D3: Most effectively absorbed UV rays from the sun into your skin but can also be found in some foods and dietary supplements. A study from 2018[1] links low vitamin D with miscarriage, which is why many doctors recommend checking this level and/or adding an additional 2000 IU a day to your supplements. Prenatal vitamins often don't carry enough vitamin D to cover the daily recommendation. (This test can be completed at any time.)
- MTHRF Gene: The MTHFR (methylenetetrahydrofolate reductase) provides instructions for your body to make the MTHR protein, which helps your body process folate. The body needs folate to make DNA and modify proteins. If you have a mutated MTHFR gene you may not be able to process folate, or it could affect how your blood clots and cause blood clotting concerns in pregnancy. Your doctor can test and tell which gene of MTHFR you have, which may be helpful in your next pregnancy. (This test can be completed at any time.)

These blood tests should be completed when your HCG is zero:

- Anti-Cardiolipin Antibodies: Looks for general blood clotting concerns, which can be treated with blood thinning medication during pregnancy.
- Antithrombin Activity: A blood test that looks for a specific protein in the liver that can help eliminate blood clotting and looks for general blood clotting concerns as well.
- Activated PTT: Tests for the average information when it comes to your body and coagulation. This is a test that times how long your blood takes to clot.

- Factor V Leiden Mutation: An inherited mutation in a specific protein in your blood. A positive test for this mutation is associated with during pregnancy.
- Glycoprotein 1 Antibodies, IGA, IGM, IGG: A molecule in your blood that affects your fertility and could also affect blood clotting.
- Lupus Anticoagulant: Auto-antibodies produced by the immune system that mistakenly attack certain components of the body's own cells. Treatment for this may be IVF to help in the process of fertilization and implantation of an embryo.
- Protein C Activity: Inactivates certain proteins in the blood that promote blood clotting.
- Protein S Activity: Normal activity and level protein C and protein S often indicate adequate clotting regulation.
- Prothrombin Gene Mutation: A genetic change to a protein that promotes blood clotting.

These genetic tests are sometimes included in the panel:

- Carrier Screening: Expanded Carrier Screening (ECS) is used to determine whether a parent is at risk of passing hundreds of diseases onto their children (such as Cystic Fibrosis). If both parents could be carries, then there is a greater concern.
- Karyotype Testing: A karyotype looks at the structure, number, and arrangement of chromosomes found in a sample of cells. This test may also be called a chromosome analysis and can often diagnose something called an unbalanced translocation, among many other things.

As you can see in the sidebar, a lot of this testing looks at how our blood clots, and the reason why that's such a huge focus in pregnancy loss is because during pregnancy, our blood volume increases significantly. In the first trimester, that's when our blood volume begins to increase. It's thought that between 8 and 10 weeks it's starting to steadily increase, which may explain how blood clotting can cause a first trimester miscarriage. The volume of blood increases progressively throughout pregnancy. If there's a concern with your blood clotting then it's helpful to know that ahead of time because it could indicate a reason for pregnancy loss that is preventable—but, of course, this information is not often found without pregnancy loss in the first place, so while it's preventable in the future, we cannot change the past.

With that being said, we are also humans and as we've discussed, blood volume increases significantly during pregnancy. So, even without a blood clotting diagnosis, it's still possible to have a blood clot in the wrong place, at the wrong time. If this is a concern of yours, you can always consult your doctor about over-the-counter medications that help avoid blood clots as well as other pregnancy complications.

When working with a fertility specialist, you may try other procedures. Here's a list of the most commonly performed tests:

- **Hysterosonogram (HSG):** An X-ray procedure that looks at your fallopian tubes using a catheter and dye.
- **Saline Infusion Sonohysterography (SIS):** A procedure that's similar to an HSG but uses an ultrasound to visualize the uterus and its inner lining (also called the endometrium) by injecting sterile saline solution. It's used to look for abnormalities like fibroids or polyps but can also help investigate abnormal uterine bleeding or recurrent losses.
- **Hysteroscopy:** An endoscopy to look at your uterine cavity through the cervix. This can be used to remove small polyps, fibroids, and sometimes retained tissue from pregnancy loss.
- **Laparoscopy:** A more invasive procedure to look for underlying conditions that may cause infertility and recurrent pregnancy loss such as endometriosis. It may be used to remove larger polyps and fibroids as well.

◆ **ReceptivaDX Test:** An endometrial biopsy used to find if any inflammation can be found in the uterine lining. Any inflammation that is found using these tests is often related to endometriosis or endometritis. Based on the results of the testing, hormone therapy or laparoscopic surgery may be recommended.

Coping with Recurrent Losses

Coping with recurrent pregnancy loss is different from coping with a single loss because the grief becomes layered, over and over again. Each loss carries its own weight, and it also builds on the heartbreak that came before. There are so many moving parts, and there isn't a one-size-fits-all path. Some people may quickly enter the world of fertility testing, specialists, medications, and treatment plans. Others may choose to wait, or may not meet the criteria for certain interventions. All experiences are valid and emotionally complicated.

COPING TOOL #1: CREATING A LIST OF GOALS OR MILESTONES

In the days following pregnancy loss, especially recurring losses, I felt lost and overwhelmed by all of the things I needed to do to ever feel safe in another pregnancy. As someone who enjoys journaling (but tends to only journal when I'm in a state of struggle) I picked up a new notebook and decided that I would write down the steps I had to take next. This practice started something that I relied on through fertility testing, treatment cycles, subsequent pregnancies and so forth. Now I work with other women who feel that same loneliness and help them feel as though they know what's coming next. I learned that by setting small, realistic goals that I felt more aware of what my next action step was and what I could aim for next. This is the perfect coping tool because in many ways, it's also a grounding exercise. Here's what you do:

1. Start by choosing one realistic and doable goal (don't choose anything too overwhelming). Remember that there is no such thing as a goal that is too small—we can call these gentle milestones if that

feels better for you. These goals may be things like "eat breakfast" or "check in with a friend." The idea is for this to be something easy to check off of your list and feel accomplished.

2. Write down one to two goals at a time. Don't get too far ahead of yourself because it may start feeling unmanageable or overwhelming. The sweet spot, in my opinion, is doing two goals at a time so that way you can visually see the next step on your list. For example, after "eat breakfast" it might be "call fertility clinic" or "wait for the next period to start."

3. Goals aren't daily action items to accomplish (unless that's what you need) but can be more focused on your fertility journey meaning there are time periods between action items. Such as "get period back" then "call the fertility clinic."

4. Physically check off everything you accomplish. This will show your brain, "Hey look, I'm being productive and achieving things," which can be helpful to restoring hope after so much loss.

5. Celebrate every win, even the ones that seem small in the grand scheme of things.

Examples of grief-related goals:

- Drink your recommended daily intake of water
- When having a grief-filled day, go for a walk (a five-minute walk counts)
- Journal through your emotions (it doesn't have to be perfect)
- Rest without guilt

Examples of fertility-related goals:

- Document your menstrual cycle or days that are important for your doctor
- Call your clinic and request an appointment
- Complete testing for recurrent pregnancy loss
- Wait for the results of all tests
- Make a game plan with your doctor

COPING TOOL #2: GRIEF MAPPING AND HONORING EACH INDIVIDUAL LOSS

When you suffer recurrent pregnancy loss, you might find that there's rarely the opportunity to fully grieve each one on its own. The sorrow tends to pile up, often without processing each loss as a separate loss. While there is collective grief, this tool helps you focus on your immediate needs.

Grief mapping is helpful because it can be used to look at each loss as its own chapter and to grieve each. The losses might tend to overlap and dates become blurry. You're in survival mode, after all.

How to use this tool:

- Create a visual or written timeline of your pregnancies and loss experiences.
- Write a few details for each one: how far along you were, what you remember most, what support you had, what was hard, what you wish had gone differently.
- Note emotional themes: how grief showed up, what helped or didn't.
- You can draw it, write it in journal form, or create a ritual around it.
- Use this as a private ritual or something to share in therapy or with a support group.

Reflection Prompts

- How does your grief over your second (third or fourth) loss compare to your first miscarriage or loss?
- Which pregnancy loss experience was the most emotionally difficult to grieve? Why do you think that is?
- How have your experiences with medical care—testing, treatment, or the way providers have spoken to you—impacted your emotional healing? Are there parts of that experience that felt supportive? Are there parts that feel dismissive or unresolved?

CHAPTER 9

Postpartum

When you hear the word *postpartum,* it's often painting the picture of a woman who just gave birth to a living child that she gets to bring home. There's talk of baby blues and postpartum depression and she's met with sympathy and kindness when she complains about the tribulations of fresh motherhood, mixed with a range of emotions and hormones. But when someone's baby dies and they don't bring them home in the same fashion, they are met with awkwardness, stigmas, taboos, and zero information on what to expect in the coming weeks.

In society, postpartum is seen as the experience of a new mother but what it really means is you are post-pregnancy. Your body is postpartum even when your baby died in the first trimester, which is not acknowledged as often as it should be. Clients who have experienced pregnancy loss in the second, and even the third trimester, report being surprised by the lack of warning when it comes to symptoms experienced postpartum. Many doctors will mention bleeding and the possibility of lactation but they don't go into detail on the timeline or *why* it occurs.

If you felt unseen by your medical providers, or society, left without follow-up care or text messages just asking how are you feeling, you are seen here and I acknowledge that you've been through pregnancy, birth, and postpartum—just in a way that wasn't expected or planned for. Sadly, it's also a way that isn't properly cared for even in the present time and with all of the medical advances we have. This chapter covers what happens to women's bodies and minds following a miscarriage or pregnancy loss at any gestation.

Physically Healing from Pregnancy Loss

In terms of discussing the physical element of postpartum, it doesn't matter what trimester you experienced your loss in or how pregnant you were— there's a physical healing that happens to everybody. Even in the first few weeks of pregnancy, your blood volume slightly increases, the uterus stretches and grows, and the surge in hormones causes symptoms that may interrupt life as you knew it. Pregnancy loss is more than a moment in time, it's more than a few drops of blood. Even if you had zero physical ailments, to go from pregnant to no longer pregnant is a difficult transition.

Whether you have a spontaneous loss at home, an induced miscarriage, a termination for medical reasons, or a procedure such as a dilation and curettage (D&C) or a dilation and evacuation (D&E), postpartum will look similar for everyone in terms of physical healing.

From the day of your physical loss, you will bleed. The level at which you bleed varies based on the type of pregnancy loss and birth that occurs. If you have had other birthing experiences, especially if they have led to living children, then you may notice that the postpartum bleeding is similar to your previous births. This can often be a validating thing to notice, while also being frustrating that the care is noticeably different. Women can bleed anywhere from a few days following pregnancy loss to three or four weeks postpartum. The bleeding often tapers off after two weeks. When there is bleeding for longer than two weeks, you should ask your doctor about the possibility of retained products of conception (trust me, it isn't my favorite wording). This can happen due to a loss that occurs on its own or by procedure and there are many factors that make someone at a higher risk, such as shape of the uterus, type of pregnancy loss, if there was use of IVF to achieve that pregnancy, and the expertise and experience of the physician who handled your care.

If you're spotting, bleeding heavily, or not bleeding at all—all of which can be completely normal—you may experience a range of symptoms, many of which can catch you off guard. From hormone changes that cause night sweats and mood swings, postpartum hair loss, and lactation in some cases—there's a lot happening.

It's important to remember that your body must heal after pregnancy loss and even if you bleed for one week and never bleed again, your uterus is returning to its pre-pregnancy size; your blood volume goes from baseline, to triple its usual volume, then back down again; your progesterone and hormone levels are fluctuating as they level out; and you still have the pregnancy hormone HCG in your blood stream for anywhere from four- to eight-weeks post-pregnancy loss.

As a miscarriage educator and someone who has supported thousands of women through pregnancy loss, I find that the postpartum stage lasts for three to six months. The reason I say this is because in the early weeks, people experience the symptoms of hormone imbalances, bleeding, and even lactation. For multiple months after loss, there can be a change in cycles as well as hair loss, exhaustion, and fatigue, and pelvic cramping. Even as time passes, experiencing the change in the way your body feels isn't an easy thing to navigate. It's often described as cruel or unfair that these symptoms last so long. It's all the more unfair that most women are left without a warning or time to prepare for the postpartum following miscarriage or pregnancy loss.

Emotional Expectations Post-Loss

The experience of grief can feel foreign, even if you've experienced other deaths in life. A common question that I see online is, *Is this normal?* I know that feeling all too well—feeling hopeless and empty, wondering if you're the only person in the world taking the loss of a pregnancy and the dreams it represented *this* hard. Especially if you know other people who have experienced pregnancy loss and no longer seem burdened by the grief.

Coping, which is discussed in Chapter 6, begins immediately following pregnancy loss. Even though you might not feel like you are processing or coping with the experience, by surviving and moving forward, you are doing the best you can at the time. It's often more difficult in the first few weeks or months afterwards. There are a lot of milestones that might disrupt your coping and can makes you feel like you aren't moving forward. Some women fear that they are backpedaling on their coping because the emotional element of postpartum literally feels like a roller-coaster. It's a common comment from my clients; they feel that having a day where tears fell without a sense of control means they are doing terribly and not handling their loss well. The reality of grief is that it truly is complicated. Even when someone has answers or handles things well in life, each and every loss that you experience holds a different meaning and your brain can react differently each time.

> The first month, even the first three months, is difficult. You are navigating through physical and emotional shifts while also grieving and attempting to return to your everyday life. Between fluctuating hormones, you are experiencing triggers (and learning how to cope with them in real time), returning to work or your pre-pregnancy daily activities, and dealing with other people's reactions to your loss, there's a lot going on.

After an untimely birth, hormones such as your human chorionic gonadotropin (HCG) levels will immediately drop at a significant rate. However, the hormone doesn't level off for many weeks. The initial drop in hormones can be compared to "the baby blues," which are known to happen in the first few days following birth. It's known that *baby blues* can happen within the first few days following birth and resolve within three weeks post-birth. Even though you aren't bringing home a baby, you are still going to experience some similar postpartum blues, only yours is mixed with grief and lacking a rise in oxytocin.

All About the First Menstrual Period

When a woman experiences the loss of a pregnancy, her doctor will express their condolences, give her the options, manage the immediate need for care, and then tell her to call the office when she's pregnant again. One piece of information that is often missing is when she can expect her cycle to return and what will it look like.

Once your pregnancy has ended, you'll have some vaginal bleeding. You could bleed for a few days or a few weeks—there are many factors that help determine that. It's safe to assume that there will be some bleeding. There are exceptions such as experiencing the loss of a twin in a twin pregnancy where the *postpartum* element is different (since you would continue to carry the surviving twin). Another type of loss that may differ could be an ectopic pregnancy, although some people may still have vaginal bleeding. Sometimes with ectopic pregnancy, you would rely more on blood work that checks your HCG levels versus tracking your bleeding.

If you suffer loss and have vaginal bleeding after, note that this is not your period. I've heard the question asked in multiple ways and there's confusion around whether it's a period or not. In some ways, it can be thought of as a period since it's a shedding of your uterine lining; however, it's not a traditional period and I normally don't treat it as such.

Following your pregnancy loss, your body is recovering, so while your uterine lining is technically shedding (which is usually what a menstrual period is), it's also shrinking in size, releasing tissue related to pregnancy, and recovering from pregnancy hormones or hormones that are impacted by pregnancy. In terms of your fertility after loss, the "first period" is typically 30 days to six (sometimes more) weeks following the loss.

Postpartum bleeding will happen for a few days or maybe a few weeks, but shouldn't last longer than two- to three-weeks post-pregnancy loss. It may start heavy but taper to a light bleed toward the end. Then you have about a week or so free of any bleeding, this is often where people catch their breath and start to feel somewhat like themselves again. Then the first period will begin once the pregnancy hormones are all zero (HCG and progesterone, specifically). The bleeding during the menstrual cycle may be heavier than it was previously and the cramps may be more intense. That is normal and a common experience.

Hormonal Changes and Fertility After Loss

Deciding what to do after experiencing a miscarriage is rarely simple. People tend to fall into one of three paths when it comes to future fertility— some feel a strong urge to try again right away, others choose (or are advised) to take a break before trying to conceive again, and some decide not to pursue future pregnancies at all. Each of these paths is deeply personal and none of them is easy. When medical circumstances take the decision out of your hands, it can bring an added layer of grief. The truth is, there's no clear roadmap after loss, and no "right" choice—only what's right for *you*.

Hormone changes could impact you in many different ways; some of them may be temporary changes and others could be more long lasting. As discussed in the first chapter, the hormones needed to have a healthy cycle must all fall within a certain range during a specific point in your cycle. If this isn't your first pregnancy, you may have experienced this before— changes in your hormones that create new symptoms during your cycle. If the pregnancy where you experienced loss was your first pregnancy, you may be very frustrated if the hormone changes affect you.

I had a client, let's call her Lacey, who tracked her menstrual cycle religiously for years by documenting symptoms, cervical mucous changes, and basal body temperature (BBT). She also utilized blood work to check her progesterone and estrogen levels throughout her cycle. Her first pregnancy ended in a missed miscarriage at 13 weeks. Following that miscarriage, she noticed changes in her ovulation, her bleeding patterns, and symptoms. She tracked the changes for four full cycles before she noticed her cycle returning to its pre-pregnancy pattern. For her, the changes were temporary; however, they were incredibly frustrating at the time because she really wanted to get pregnant again as soon as possible. If you don't track your cycles the way Lacey did, you may not be able to catch the elements of your cycle that are different. Tracking these changes after loss can be useful for your medical team if you need additional medical support while trying to conceive again.

It's important to remember that a pregnancy itself will not make you *more* fertile nor will it take away your fertility. It does impact your cycle and it could reduce the chance of pregnancy unless you track your cycle very closely. In the big picture, being pregnant and experiencing loss does not make or break your fertility. At least not without an explanation or specific concern.

Reflection Prompts

- ◆ Do you relate to feeling *postpartum* after pregnancy loss? Why or why not?
- ◆ During the first six weeks following your loss, what aspect of healing (or postpartum) was most difficult for you?
- ◆ Have you noticed any changes to your menstrual cycle?

CHAPTER 10

Moving Forward (Not Moving On)

I am of the opinion that life after loss is where we all are for days, months, and years to come following pregnancy loss. When I first suffered a miscarriage, I couldn't wait until I was out of the grief and no longer on a "pregnancy loss journey." As time has passed, over six years as I write this book, I've learned that we are forever living "life after loss" just as we are always going to grieve the people we lose in life, the babies that never made it earth-side and the experience of physically losing them will always be a part of our story.

Life after loss can include many different directions including prioritizing emotional healing, seeing specialists or counselors that can help with diagnosis related to your loss experience, trying to conceive again and navigating pregnancy after loss, and so forth. There are endless ways our lives can unfold; some moments will feel uplifting and hopeful, and others may bring added stress and despair. That's why I like to say that miscarriage or pregnancy loss itself doesn't end when the bleeding stops—or when the physical miscarriage is over. The effects of pregnancy loss are everlasting and while they change shapes over time, they still exist.

After experiencing pregnancy loss, you may find yourself wondering *when* you'll feel like yourself again. And from reading this book—you probably know that I'm about to tell you that we may never go back to who we were *before*. The *previous* version of yourself is a different version of who you are right now. It's okay to mourn the loss of your naive, pre-loss self. It's actually crucial to moving forward and learning to carry your grief with you. I call this *the new normal* and it's not ideal, but it is the reality of experiencing pregnancy loss. Basically, you're having to get to know yourself again and that's not what you planned for.

Following my first miscarriage, I knew that something had changed and that my personality had shifted, the emotional bandwidth that I carried was smaller, and that everything about me was different. The hard part was that I also knew that people wouldn't be able to tell from just looking at me. It was a deeper shift that people may only notice in conversation or by spending long periods of time with me. My ability to have "small talk" became nonexistent and while I was introverted prior to pregnancy loss, I was far more fearful of exerting my social battery. The way that I described this change with myself was by referring to it as my *new normal*. Truth be told, I wasn't ready to admit that my miscarriage probably changed me and that I would never get to be my old self again. So, labeling this as a new normal felt more comfortable.

Now, who's to say that someone can't have a miscarriage or a later-term loss and feel like themselves within days, weeks, or months? That does happen and sometimes the feeling of being lost is temporary—and if it's not a fleeting feeling then getting to know this version of yourself is next in moving forward following pregnancy loss at any gestation. Another crucial aspect of moving forward is honoring how you feel and trying to do so without judgment (from yourself and others). It's not abnormal to feel like yourself soon after loss but it's also not abnormal to not feel like yourself. We truly cannot know how our brain will react to loss, which is why I always tell people the worst-case scenarios (and mention the best cases too!).

Chances are, you picked up this book because you are struggling with your grief in one way or another so moving forward isn't an easy task for you. This huge shift has occurred and life suddenly looks different than it *should*, so—naturally—you're feeling really crappy. Since we've talked about grief, trauma, triggers, relationships, postpartum, and so forth, let's map out the rest of this version of healing and help you actually move forward in a way that doesn't leave your loss behind, but also doesn't weigh you down.

Throughout this book, we've highlighted how language is important and the words we use to describe the events of our lives are impactful in our grief. I often hear people express that they are feeling inadequate in their grief because they "aren't over it yet" and it breaks my heart that anyone thinks they will just move on from what's happened to them and the immense loss that they've experienced.

I believe that this comes from a generational difference in how we speak about personal matters such as pregnancy loss, because the generations before us did not talk about it when it happened to them. Miscarriage, stillbirth, and talking about menstrual cycles have been taboo for entirely too long and *not* talking about it is what helps build the stigma that surrounds it. Language that suggests we should *move on* after a traumatic experience builds up the walls that I so desperately want to knock down because most people won't move on, they won't get over their grief, and they won't find that another pregnancy replaces the pain of their loss experience.

This is why the sentiment of moving forward is so meaningful to me. I needed someone to tell me that I could feel my grief and continue forward in my fertility journey and that I didn't need to move on, at least not yet.

Moving forward doesn't mean that we are forgetting or replacing the child that we've lost, the pregnancy that didn't continue, the dreams that we dreamt. It means that we are learning to live in a world that no longer looks how we imagined or planned for. "Moving on" implies leaving something behind, getting over it, forgetting about it altogether. It also highlights the shame around feeling grief even though we have no control over how heavy grief feels and for how long we feel it. To refer to life after loss and the survival of grief as *moving forward* allows you to carry your baby's memory with you and it recognizes that grief doesn't disappear.

You deserve space and time to grieve without the expectation that you should be healed at all, let alone on a timeline.

Processing and Acknowledging Grief

The day that my first pregnancy was confirmed as a missed miscarriage, I immediately thought about my employer and how I would handle the projects that I had at work while also managing a life-altering experience. Then I thought of my closest friend who was pregnant and three weeks ahead of my own pregnancy. Everything was going well for her, and she was so supportive of me at that time, but my mind went to how I would have to continue watching her pregnancy progress while my world was stopped at a standstill. In the years that followed my miscarriages, I started working as a bereavement doula and learned that disassociation often happens in that moment because of the traumatic event. Nothing was more important than my pregnancy, especially since my life wasn't in danger. But I couldn't help but try to find excuses as to why I *couldn't* handle a miscarriage. Even though, ready or not, a miscarriage was happening.

I spent three days in what I referred to as a *grief bubble*. My husband and I stayed home, ordered take-out, and felt the immense sadness that was the reality of losing our first baby. But there were moments where I wondered if it were all a dream. Did the doctor really say that we were having a miscarriage? Did he seem certain? Could he be wrong? Even though I understood what was said to me, I couldn't fully process it at that time. Now that I support so many other women while they navigate through the very experience I had, and having six years between my first pregnancy and today, I see that it was difficult for me to fully process the miscarriage until the physical aspect of loss was complete.

Accepting that your baby has died, that your pregnancy has ended, that you essentially have to get pregnant again—possibly spending a lot of money to achieve that—is no easy feat. It doesn't happen overnight and even if you're someone who is doing *all of the things* to cope, some wounds take more than time to heal. Healing itself is never done, because you don't just move on from the experience unchanged. But it does get easier over time.

When you are processing grief, there's not often an ah-ha moment where you just *know* that your brain has fully comprehended the magnitude of what you've lost and how it impacts you. Sometimes the reality of death and grief isn't understood until years later, which again is why it's difficult to "feel better," which is what I think a lot of people are expecting from the work that's detailed in this book regarding grief. We should look at this experience for what it is, something that's happened to our lives. It can't be changed or taken away, and acknowledging that truth will give some freedom to the lack of control we often feel following pregnancy loss.

If you've been avoiding the processing element of grief, this is your friendly nudge that you can't avoid it forever. At some point, you have to acknowledge what's happened and then create a path forward. That's not to say that this has to be done right away in order to not let the grief of loss weigh you down. When you feel ready to conquer the difficult elements of your pregnancy experience, the topics in this chapter can help you navigate through the dark days of life after loss.

BASIC STEPS TO BEGIN PROCESSING LOSS

As much as I wish I could hand you a "get over your miscarriage quick" package, grief just doesn't work that way. When we begin to process a death or traumatic event, that's when the so-called healing begins. We begin finding the tools that help us navigate through the valleys of grief and lead us through difficult times.

First, Acknowledge Your Loss

When it comes to processing any life experience that is world-altering, such as pregnancy loss, the first step is to acknowledge the loss and the impact of the grief on your life. It sounds simple to say "I had a miscarriage" but the reality is much more complicated than that and that's only the beginning. To acknowledge your loss means to accept that you were pregnant and now aren't and that as life moves forward, you have to find ways to move forward as well.

In many ways, this goes back to John Bowlby's theory on the stages of grief (discussed in Chapter 3).[1] His model focused on his attachment theory. Bowlby's attachment theory basically points out that a child is born with the innate drive to form attachments and then as adults, those attachments shape our relationships and abilities as we move throughout life. Part of his belief in the grief of losing a child is that we, as the pregnant person, see that child as an extension of ourselves. Losing a child disrupts a parent's sense of purpose, identity, and safety in the world, all of which are tied to their internal working model shaped by attachment.

One thing that I appreciate about John Bowlby's work on attachment and the death of someone that we have formed attachment with is that there is no replacement for that bond. Even if you have another pregnancy and that pregnancy leads to another child, the bond and connection are different even if in the slightest of ways.

With the knowledge that you are grieving an attachment that is more like a bond, the hope is that you have a better understanding of why it's difficult to process what's happened to you. There are so many people who assume they aren't grieving correctly—or in a healthy way—but that's not always the case.

Acknowledging your pregnancy loss might look like:

- *Saying it out loud:* As silly as it sounds, looking at yourself in the mirror and telling yourself that you've suffered the loss of your pregnancy in whatever terminology feels most comfortable for yourself can be helpful.
- *Journaling:* Whether on a daily, weekly, or monthly basis, journaling is a great way to check in with yourself and hold space for your grief.
- *If it feels right for you, naming your baby:* A deeply personal decision and one that doesn't come easily for many—naming your baby is helpful in coping with the grief of losing them.
- *Creating a ritual:* Planting flowers in a garden or a tree, lighting a candle on the day of the week where your gestation would shift, or doing something in their memory.
- *Talking to someone about your loss:* A friend, people in a support group, a therapist, talking about your experience with pregnancy loss and the grief that you're experiencing is incredibly helpful to navigating the future after your loss.

One of these actions might be enough for you to feel the acceptance of death and sometimes it takes doing one or more of these processing tools to fully grasp how much has changed in a short amount of time. Remember that acknowledging your loss and creating space for those emotions doesn't mean you're over it in any sense of the word. It's necessary to acknowledge grief; that way you can cope with it—not get over it. Be patient with yourself and find ways to support that connection even in death.

Next, Find Space for Your Loss

For so many people, this stage of processing their miscarriage is the most difficult because it doesn't come naturally to everyone nor does every person have the support of a significant other or family and friends. Consider these ideas:

+ *Joining a support group (or going on a podcast):* Talking about your miscarriage or pregnancy loss experience with other people is extremely helpful.
+ *Making time and space for tangible items:* Depending on the type of pregnancy loss that's experienced, there may or may not be tangible items to remember your baby. These items could be ultrasound photos, hospital bracelets, clothes that you purchased for them, or positive pregnancy tests from when you first learned that you were pregnant. If you do have mementos or items that belonged to your baby or from your pregnancy, creating a space in your home to showcase as much as you're comfortable with is a positive step in acknowledging what's happened and that your baby is no longer with you. You may have a shelf in your bedroom, or a common area. Making space for your baby's stuff helps your brain understand that even though they aren't here with you, you can still care for them in your own way. If you do not have tangible items, purchasing ornaments, figurines, t-shirts, and more can be helpful especially if you didn't get the chance to make any purchases or collect any ultrasound photos.

Creating space for your grief can be a deeply personal experience where you find things that help you feel like you're mothering—or parenting— the child that you've lost. In some practices, putting 15 minutes on a timer and taking that time to honor your pregnancy, think about the life that should still be within you, journaling, or even just lighting a candle is sufficient on a daily or weekly basis.

> The important thing is not necessarily *how* you spend time grieving but that you ensure you're making the space and taking up that space, too.

Then, Discuss Your Loss with People You Trust

A common misconception is that you have to tell everyone in your life about the struggles you're facing in life. Let's say that you're someone who has a friend group where there are five or more people, you have a group chat, and see each other often. I imagine that there is a lot of pressure to share the same information with all of those people. This might be why people share things in a group chat, even if they would prefer not to share with everyone. There's a pressure to be a *good friend* and share things with everyone, without prioritizing one friend over another.

The reality is that you get to choose who you share such personal information with. Not everyone deserves to know your story and not everyone deserves to know about your pregnancy experience either. Whether you have a group of friends or a few close friends that you trust, the choice of how (or if) you share is yours to make.

A few things to know about discussing your loss with people you trust:

- ◆ You're allowed to discuss your pregnancy loss experience through text messaging if that's more comfortable for you! I know that when we have big news to share—both good and bad—or when we are struggling and want to reach out for support, we feel like it has to be a formal phone call but it doesn't necessarily need to be. It depends on your comfort level and which form of communication you'd prefer with your trusted support person.

◆ Don't be afraid to tell your people *what* would feel best for you. Would you like for them to check in with you on a regular basis—like once a week at minimum—and are you more comfortable with text message, video call, or phone call? Or do you want them to hold off on bringing up your miscarriage and wait for you to bring it up in conversation before checking in and giving you space? Communicate your needs so they can support you wholly.

◆ Sometimes we have to create our own support system through joining a support group—virtual or in person—or making friends in online grief spaces. These are all good options in seeking support and finding trusted people to talk about your loss experience with. There are also podcasts that focus on fertility issues, pregnancy loss, and grief where you can share your story if you'd like to openly share your story on a bigger platform (which is also helpful in processing grief).

BREAKING STIGMAS

Prior to experiencing pregnancy loss, we are aware that people all over the world experience miscarriage but we aren't properly informed on the statistics and the risk of loss during a pregnancy. As a society, we know that people announce their pregnancies publicly on social media after the 12th week and if we notice they share the news early, there's often judgment for sharing too early. But when we break down these social norms that we've created and upheld in our society then we may realize that we are part of a machine that creates the stigma for pregnant people. Oftentimes, it's not until it affects us personally that we realize how damaging these stigmas are.

Many women, including myself, experience pregnancy loss and immediately want to break down the walls of the stigma that surrounds them.

It's a common reaction to experiencing something that happens privately but feels too big, too life-changing, not to speak out about.

So how do you move forward in a way that honors your experience, protects your peace, and helps break the stigma for people of the future who will have pregnancy loss? Just like anything else, there is no magic formula but little by little, you can help normalize the grief and trauma that comes with having a miscarriage or losing a pregnancy—a child—in any trimester.

- *Educate yourself on all things related to pregnancy and loss.* Reproductive rights, healthcare, access to funding for studies, are all helpful things to know as you navigate through life after loss but are also helpful in breaking down the taboo walls that surround pregnancy loss. The more we know, the more we can help others and discuss reproductive healthcare.
- *Share your story whenever you feel comfortable doing so.* While it may not seem like something that can make the biggest difference, the art of storytelling does wonders in our world revolving around challenging conversations or topics that are uncomfortable in nature.

Re-entering the World After Loss

After experiencing pregnancy loss, the world never looks the same. You become acutely aware of how life carries on unchanged for those around you, even as everything has shifted through your eyes. When someone loses a pregnancy or a baby that they planned for and had dreams of, the future is uncertain. How does someone re-enter a world that to the naked eye looks the same but feels completely different? It's not simple nor is it easy.

DEALING WITH NEW FIRSTS

Re-entering the world consists of many milestones or events that take place following a major life event, more commonly discussed following a death because grief is unique and subjective to each individual and their experience. When I'm working with clients and we are creating a plan for moving forward, we often include the *firsts,* which consist of events such as returning to work, attending a baby shower, having a full menstrual cycle, or being intimate with your partner following loss. The list may change based on someone's personal life and the social battery they possess but this is the general blueprint that I've found helpful for grieving people. All of these events are things that we do or take part in to try and re-enter the world or live life as we did prior to loss. For some people, it might be a helpful distraction but for others it's triggering and difficult to commit to.

Inside someone's mind, they could have racing thoughts wondering *What went wrong?* or *Where would I be today if my baby hadn't died?* And as they have this internal struggle between grief, shame, blame, jealousy, and anger, they see that the outside world is unchanged by their loss and everything is essentially the same—even though to them, it looks and feels very different.

Another layer to attempting to go back to the life you lived prior to your pregnancy ending without a baby in your arms, is that there is a pressure to be *okay* or to be able to leave your personal struggles at home and wear a mask at work or in a busy social environment. The thought process comes from the work force and from previous generations because we are told not to bring our personal business into our job or to discuss personal issues with others. That's where the shame comes in and the continued stigmatization of pregnancy loss in general. For people who don't want to hide their emotions or struggles, this can be really uncomfortable, which is unfortunate because they are already going through so much that shame or embarrassment is not needed.

RETURNING TO WORK

Returning to work is a huge stressor for many people who have experienced a death or severe trauma. One aspect is depending on where you live and the benefits that you have with your employer. The United States doesn't have mandatory bereavement leave or mandatory parental leave. However, time off regardless of gestation is important for everyone. Birthing partners or their non-birthing partners alike.

Following my first miscarriage, I was given two weeks off of work, which isn't normal and I was very grateful for that time. Truth be told, I could have used more time but didn't feel comfortable asking for it and also wanted some feeling of normalcy. I also didn't know about the FMLA (Family and Medical Leave Act), which in in the United States is protection for people who take unpaid time from work for issues like recovery from pregnancy loss. If someone meets the qualifications, which can be found on the U.S. Department of Labor's website, they may be entitled to up to 12 weeks of protection. Most grieving people are craving to feel like themselves again and it's not until we take these steps to go out into the world that we realize how different the world is for us now.

The day that I returned to work after that miscarriage was painful and I felt completely caught off guard by how difficult it was. Parking my car in the designated parking spot that I had parked in for years prior, everything felt different and I couldn't understand that feeling nor did I fully recognize it at the time. Then walking into the office and setting down my belongings at my desk, I started to cry. This desk is where the old version of myself sat for eight hours a day, five days a week. She would search for baby nursery themes, eat snacks throughout the day, listen to podcasts on motherhood and pregnancy. The version of myself that existed prior to losing my first child was no longer the person sitting in that same chair and preparing for the same day, at the same job. It hit me then that the last time I sat in that chair, I was still pregnant. While my baby wasn't alive, they were with me and inside of my body. Air completely left my lungs, and I struggled to breathe as I processed just how different my work life felt now that I went from being pregnant to no longer being pregnant.

Now when I talk to people about returning to work following pregnancy loss, I realize that this is a shared experience. Unfortunately, none of us feel like ourselves anymore. Many of us are desperately trying to find that older version of ourselves or to understand this new version. It's difficult because you don't know future outcomes either and there's no promise of a reward for your suffering.

BEING SOCIAL

Another aspect of re-entering the world is attending social events, gatherings with friends or family, or just going out into the world in general. Just as we discussed returning to work, doing anything that you did before with ease and realizing how different it feels now—is painful at baseline. Whether there are people in your support system who know what you've been through or not, it's not likely that they fully understand and this leaves room for error while you're grieving.

A discussion that I have often with other bereaved parents is how the triggers that we process and identify are everywhere. It's almost a guarantee that every time you leave your home, you'll see a pregnant person or a mother with young kids. I know from experience that you can't help but wonder *how* she got to where she is. Did she experience loss too? Is this her "rainbow baby"? Or did she struggle with infertility? When this takes place, I truly believe that it's coming from seeking validation, relatability, and looking for hope as well.

There are layers to attending any kind of social gathering or event following pregnancy loss. Whenever the topic has come up in one of our grief support groups there is a portion of the discussion that focuses on protecting your peace and not going to something that will be upsetting or triggering, and another part of the conversation is on processing the experience will be difficult and different but not an impossible task. Finding your place again in a world that no longer feels the same often means seeking out tools that help you cope with grief and move through it, one step at a time.

Reflection Prompts

A useful challenge for yourself may be to sit and write down the *firsts* or times when you expect re-entering the world to be difficult.

- What event is taking place?
- How are you anticipating that you'll feel getting out of that comfort zone?
- What tools can you use to support yourself?
- Have you created a disaster plan (so to speak)?

Navigating the Opinions (and Words) of Others

We live in a society where people are uncomfortable with things like death and somehow unable to filter insensitive comments and unsolicited advice when someone has experienced a death and is grieving. As someone who lives and breathes grief (not only because of a job choice but because I've dealt with a lot of it), I cannot make sense of the things that people will say to a bereaved parent.

I was not prepared for the words and phrases that people used as an attempt to comfort me. Some extended family members said things like "maybe it wasn't their time" or "at least your loss happened early" and it was incredibly hurtful. The first interaction that I had like that came from a nurse at my fertility clinic and I had just learned that my body was 11 weeks pregnant but the pregnancy itself was measuring six weeks. She meant well but her words were hurtful and in the early stages of my loss, I took what she said and thought about it for weeks. Why wasn't my baby good enough to be here with me? When would be a better time for them to exist? Should I not feel so sad since people experience loss later than I have?

As bereaved parents or bereaved people, whichever represents you best, it's important that we walk into grief knowing that there truly is no silver lining. Nothing anyone could say will make our loss any lighter or any easier. It's okay to acknowledge how difficult the grief feels and how unfair or unjust pregnancy loss is to our lives. We do not have to have a positive attitude in order to heal from something devastating—don't let anyone tell you otherwise.

Remember three things about the words of other people as you navigate this grief:

- ◆ People can have good intentions but still cause you pain with their words or their actions.
- ◆ Boundaries might be uncomfortable but necessary for a period of time.
- ◆ You don't owe anyone an explanation surrounding your grief, its timeline, or its intensity. Let people make assumptions if they must— it's your journey not theirs.

Forgiving Your Body

Body image is not something that women are strangers to because the way we look has been a focus of our lives since puberty. It's engrained in our society to push specific messages such as "bouncing back" or having a flat stomach, perfect breasts, the list goes on. In pregnancy, so many women struggle with their body from the get-go because there's bloating, there's discomfort, and we don't feel our best. In a full-term pregnancy, that only gets heavier on the mental load because the body changes *a lot*.

ACKNOWLEDGING THE CHANGES

What people may not realize is that pregnancy can change our body from the very beginning. Whether we're nauseous so we aren't eating as much, we are bloated and look like we've already gained 15 pounds, or if we have a smaller torso and actually start showing in pregnancy earlier than others—there are a lot of ways for the body to look and feel different even in the first trimester. Something else that isn't widely discussed under this topic is how someone can have pregnancy symptoms (such as the bloating or weight gain) while experiencing a miscarriage. This happens more in missed miscarriages or second/third trimester losses where the uterus has started to expand—this happens roughly 7 weeks into pregnancy—so someone may look or feel pregnant even if their baby is no longer alive. It's a cruel, horrible joke that's placed on those people and it happens more often than you may realize.

Following pregnancy loss, there are many struggles that are top of mind and the way we feel about our body is usually a top contender but it's not voiced as often as other problems. How can you explain to someone that you don't necessarily blame yourself for your miscarriage but you're really ticked off at your body because it gave you no warning signs and kept growing the pregnancy like everything was okay. Or if you're someone who struggled with infertility first, you probably were already really frustrated with your body. There are many ways that we can feel let down or disappointed by our body due to fertility struggles and it's not easy to come back from.

If you're struggling with forgiving your body for your loss, trusting your body with future menstrual cycles or pregnancies, feeling safe or comfortable with your body—you are not alone. This is grief and it's complicated. Think of it this way, life and death have happened within your body but you're having to live through and survive that death. Who else are we going to blame? We often feel self-blame in one way or another but our body takes the brunt of the blame and that often feels justified because our body was supposed to choose the healthiest egg and sperm and grow a beautiful, healthy baby but it didn't and whether or not we know why this happened—we are allowed to feel angry.

Finding a sense of peace or forgiveness with your body after pregnancy loss can be incredibly difficult. But with time and intention, you can begin to reconnect with yourself in meaningful ways.

BODY CONNECTION PRACTICE

This practice can help you begin to reconnect with your body in meaningful ways:

1. Find a quiet, comfortable place. You can either lie flat on your back in bed or on the floor. Close your eyes and begin to breathe slowly and deeply. With each breath, bring your awareness to different parts of your body. You might start at your fingertips and slowly work your way down to your toes, or move in whatever order feels natural to you.

2. Some people may choose to focus specifically on the pelvic area—where so much pain and anger can be held. That's what I did after my first miscarriage. I needed to give that part of my body space to be seen, felt, and grieved.

3. While you do this, focus on simply being present with your body—not trying to change anything or fix it, but allowing yourself to feel. You might play calming music or sit in silence. This practice combines mindfulness, breathwork, and emotional release.

4. Try it for just 5–10 minutes at a time. Let this be a moment of honoring what your body has carried, lost, and endured.

Reflection Prompts

- ◆ What emotions do you hold in your body when thinking about your losses?
- ◆ Are there specific areas where you feel tension, grief, or blame? Imagine what it would feel like to offer those parts compassion and understanding instead of criticism and anger.

GETTING TO KNOW YOURSELF AGAIN

The first step to getting to know yourself post-loss is to acknowledge that you are a different person than the version of yourself that hadn't experienced the loss of your child, or pregnancy. It's not a simple thing to accept and for so many women, it takes time.

One aspect of life after loss that people struggle with is finding joy in hobbies or activities that once boosted their mental health. Feeling joy when you're grieving can be confusing and riddled with guilt but it's necessary to find things that still help you feel happy because the pre-loss version of yourself may be felt in those moments of joy.

You're not a lost soul who will never return to its body; you've experienced a grave loss that has impacted every aspect of your life and it's difficult to come back from that without any scars or battle wounds.

Here are some actions you can take in finding yourself after loss and reconnecting with yourself:

- Carve out time on the same day, every week to do something good for yourself. Prioritize things that make you feel good, healthy, beautiful, and refreshed.
- Schedule date nights (or days) with your partner (if applicable) or a good friend and use that time to connect over things outside of your grief, play 20 questions while you wait for your meal, go to a trivia night, or watch a movie that neither of you have seen before.
- Write a list of things that are important to you (people, things, places, memories) as a way to remind yourself that you are not a complete stranger. This practice will allow you to visualize the ways that you are the same person while giving grace to your grieving self. It's also a helpful list to have on hard grief-filled days.

Communicating Long-Term Grief to Others

People in your life may not understand the extent of this grief and the loss (or losses) that you've experienced. There will likely be a comment or two about how you're *still sad* or asking you when you will *move on* and the truth is that anyone who hasn't experienced this type of grief cannot possibly understand its weight.

Boundaries are very important as you continue to move through grief and it's unfortunate because, most of the time, they are incredibly uncomfortable to set and hold with people in your life. Some grieving people may set those immediately following their pregnancy loss, while others will set them if needed. We are always hopeful that they aren't needed and sometimes we simply don't know what our support will look like and if we will need to advocate for ourselves.

The reason why boundaries come up so often in grief is because grief itself is emotionally, mentally, and physically demanding. When our energy is already spent on something that we didn't ask for nor did we want, everything else feels too overwhelming. Setting boundaries with people in your life—or even yourself—is crucial to your emotional well-being as you move through grief.

Well-meaning family members, friends, neighbors, acquaintances, can still say something that unintentionally causes hurt or pain. The truth is that most people don't know what to say, so they say the wrong thing while meaning it to be helpful or loving.

Communicating your grief in a long-term form to others can look like:

- "Before I [show up for an event], I wanted to reach out and let you know that the past few [days/weeks/months] have been incredibly difficult for me. If I seem distant or emotional, it's not personal, I'm going through a lot at the moment. I may leave early if I feel that it's too hard to be in a social environment and want to give you the heads up."
- "Just because time has passed doesn't mean I'm over what happened. This loss is something I carry with me every day, even if I don't always talk about it."
- "Please do not ask me about getting pregnant after loss. I'm focusing on my grief at the moment and if I have news to share about our family building plans, I'll share when I'm ready."

◆ "There are certain times of year or topics that still hit hard for me. Please don't take it personally if I step away or need space. It's just part of how I cope with this loss."

Feeling Multiple Emotions at Once

Moving forward after pregnancy loss is filled with conflicting emotions, which is often an added stressor to the grieving people. If you haven't experienced other types of grief or loss that have impacted your life to an inkling of this degree, then you may be new to the feeling of "two emotions at once" where both emotions feel loud and present while also combating the other.

In the online infertility community, when I spent time there many years ago, we used to say "I'm happy for you but sad for me" when we learned that someone was pregnant. I find that it's still relevant with pregnancy loss because it highlights the fact that we can (and do) express multiple emotions at one time.

One of the hardest parts of grieving in the context of fertility and reproductive health is that you rarely get a break from it. Just as you're trying to process your loss, you're often pulled right back into the world of family building, making it nearly impossible to set the grief down, even for a moment. Which means there's grief while you're also trying to remain hopeful that your next pregnancy will have a different outcome. Then there are also people who are navigating this grief on top of the grief that comes with no longer being able to try and conceive for another pregnancy. Either way, navigating grief while trying to find joy and hope in life is incredibly difficult.

Many of the women I meet will tell me that they feel *hopeless* but then I watch them continue moving forward whether that's through seeing their doctor, trying to conceive again, planning a vacation as a coping mechanism, starting therapy to process their past—and all of these things show that there is hope in a better future. Even when we *feel* hopeless, we often aren't lacking hope at all. It's that we are afraid to let that hope be known. After pregnancy loss, there's this fear of jinxing things, such as a cycle, or another pregnancy, and it's baseless; however, it's how we attempt to cope with the fear of further devastation.

An emotion that comes up, particularly when someone is pregnant following pregnancy loss, is guilt. There's a fear of enjoying pregnancy because that means you're betraying the child that you've lost, and there are heavy emotions around planning, preparing, and dreaming of another life. I label this as "parent guilt" and although we often talk about this in the context of *mom guilt* revolving around a mother with living children, I see similar scenarios through the lens of pregnancy loss all the time. It's the same as having two children and being afraid to love one more than the other. Being pregnant after loss feels a lot like that—trying to even out the love and excitement that you give to each pregnancy, except one pregnancy lasts longer (hopefully much longer and full-term) compared to the first one.

Looking Forward to Future Pregnancies

Whether you've had one miscarriage, a loss at a later gestation, termination for medical reasons, or multiple losses, you will likely approach the topic of future pregnancies at some point. It's not uncommon—or abnormal—to be fearful and hopeful at the same time. It's an aspect of this journey—or quest as I've been calling it—that has different pathways and destinations.

Some women immediately think about future pregnancies and what that experience could be like following a miscarriage, while others need more space and distance from their fertility before trying to conceive again. There is no right or wrong way to navigate the complexity of grieving while attempting to make plans, or hopeful predictions on how future pregnancies could go—and preparations based on those hopes.

What can you do to prepare yourself for the hardship of trying to conceive again and potentially being pregnant? I'll tell you that my approach was to just try and conceive, without preparing myself, and I truly thought that pregnancy would heal everything. If I could just get pregnant and stay pregnant, nothing else would matter. Does that sound like a thought that you've had, too? The reason why I went into bereavement work is because the reality of pregnancy after loss was so far from what I had expected, and I wish that I'd had someone who told me the things that I now share with my clients.

COMMON QUESTIONS

Let's answer some of the most common questions that I see when I poll my community or meet with clients.

- ◆ **How do you know when you're ready to try to conceive again?**
  There is no guideline for the emotional and mental load of navigating your family-building desires or fertility following pregnancy loss and, sadly, there's no lightbulb moment when you know that you're emotionally ready to welcome a new pregnancy. It's a difficult thing to navigate because no one, not even you, has the answers to a question that feels so massive and important. Physically, you're usually ready following the first menstrual cycle that follows pregnancy loss—unless a medical professional has advised you otherwise. It's important for you to know that being physically cleared to get pregnant again does not mean that you *have* to get pregnant right now. There are special circumstances that make us (women) feel like we have to rush into another pregnancy and it's often timing, age, or outside factors that impact our family. If you are free of those burdens, then you have that freedom to wait until you feel emotionally and mentally comfortable with another pregnancy. Even then, you may not ever feel 100% ready and that is *normal*. After experiencing pregnancy loss, no one feels excited about another pregnancy and if they are excited, it's the type that's also mixed with fear. Again, these are all normal responses to what they've experienced.

◆ **At what point in a pregnancy following loss will I feel less anxiety?** The roadmap to pregnancy after loss is customized for each and every person who is pregnant following loss and there are parts of the map that are blank because we cannot predict how we will feel at any gestation in the next pregnancy. It's yet another unfair aspect of how grief truly has no blueprint and no one can help us bypass the difficult parts of life after loss. Some people feel heightened anxiety during the first half of the pregnancy, depending on when their previous pregnancy ended. For so many people, getting past the point they made it to with their last pregnancy is helpful and they start to feel calmer. There's also the chance that you're anxious throughout pregnancy and that's completely understandable. Pregnancy is nothing like we see in the movies and it creates the illusion that some people truly enjoy every minute of their pregnancy. While there may be people out there, it's not the majority whatsoever. Pregnancy is hard. Go easy on yourself in your next pregnancy. Acknowledge the anxiety and fear but also allow yourself to complain about the hardships, or feel good about enjoying pregnancy, if you're someone who does!

◆ **Are there ways to *stay positive* while fighting the fear and anxiety of being pregnant again?** It *is* possible to have positive thoughts and feel good about your next pregnancy. While many people fear that pregnancy itself will be difficult after loss, that's something based on fear because of our experiences. There's nothing wrong with having fears nor is there anything wrong with going into a pregnancy expecting the worst—it's how your brain is processing pregnancy, loss, then pregnancy again. What I see happen the most is that people will grieve the whole pregnancy experience following a loss, then they rightfully feel anxious in the beginning of pregnancy. Many people feel a relief that follows entering the second trimester (or a specific milestone) and then they are able to enjoy elements of pregnancy that they didn't expect to experience. There's no one-size-fits-all approach to pregnancy or pregnancy loss; therefore, a lot of what we think or feel is based on fear. Sometimes reality is different (maybe even better) than we had anticipated and sometimes that's what pregnancy after loss is like.

◆ **How can my medical team support me in my next pregnancy, which may be different from previous ones?** A great proactive step to take in your own healthcare following pregnancy loss is to request a follow-up appointment—unless one is given to you without needing to request—and discuss your physical recovery as well as what your doctor thinks went "wrong" and what they can offer you during your next pregnancy. Personally, when working with clients, we create a "pregnancy plan" which lays out the support that we are desiring and that could look like:

● Requesting a blood draw to get your human chorionic gonadotropin (HCG) hormones checked following a positive pregnancy test. This number is important and most useful when you repeat the blood draw 48–72 hours after the first one. That way the doctor can compare the levels and determine if there's any risk of early pregnancy loss or an ectopic pregnancy. In some losses, this is the first sign that things aren't going well so it could bring bad news or encouragement.

● Discussing the benefits of an early ultrasound to rule out an ectopic pregnancy but also to get a *baseline* look at your pregnancy; that way you can compare to a later ultrasound (usually two weeks later) to ensure that growth is on track and looks good. This is especially important if you've had a missed miscarriage—then you may want to have your second ultrasound around the time of your loss, when your pregnancy stopped growing, or just to see that they are in fact growing. A common practice in pregnancy is to have two or three ultrasounds during the entire pregnancy and that doesn't have to be the reality for you especially if you'd like more ultrasounds. Never hesitate to set boundaries or wishes, especially with your medical team. It's okay to ask for more or less of what they are offering you.

◆ **Will I feel guilty if I enjoy my next pregnancy even though I'll always miss the baby I've lost?** Feeling guilt is an unfortunate byproduct of grief. Moving forward and through life means that at times you'll feel joy, you might laugh at a joke, and enjoy a date night with your partner. But it also means there will be days filled with grief where you'd rather not face the day. Pregnancy after loss can bring up these emotions and internal conflicts because you are constantly feeling multiple things at one time. Yes, you'll feel guilt for loving another baby, for enjoying a moment with them, maybe even a moment you didn't get with the baby or babies you've lost. When those moments come, remind yourself that you can be happy for what you have and sad for what you've lost and oftentimes those emotions happen at the same time.

Grieving the End of Your Fertility Journey

Unfortunately, not every fertility journey will end with a living child and it's a hard reality that we often don't hear discussed. There are various reasons why someone may stop trying to conceive or be unable to conceive following pregnancy loss and it could be related to an already identified fertility diagnosis, age, life goals paired with age, financial capabilities for fertility treatment, or lack of success with fertility treatment in general.

Grief comes up with all things; infertility, pregnancy loss, baby loss, the loss of a relationship or friendship. It's no different when there's a major life decision that you either make or have made for you.

I have a client, we'll call her Katherine. Katherine decided that she wanted to wait until she was 35 years old to have children because within her workforce, she had goals on that she wanted to achieve before having a family. The tricky part, at 35 she was single and not seriously dating anyone. This caused her to have the *if it happens, it happens* thought process. Katherine thought that if she didn't have children, she would be okay and maybe not meeting someone until later was a sign that she shouldn't have them.

(continued)

Luck would have it that when Katherine was 36 years old she met the person that she was going to marry a year and a half later at 37 years old. Once they were married, they started trying to conceive right away. Months and months went by and all of Katherine's pregnancy tests were negative. She was defeated and worried that now she would never be a mother and while she was fine with the idea when it was just her—she wanted to build a family with her husband. They got pregnant when she was 38 years old—her age is an important element in this specific story—and were over-the-moon excited for the opportunity to be parents. At 12 weeks of pregnancy, Katherine and her partner learned that they were having a missed miscarriage and that she would need a D&C as soon as possible.

Katherine was devastated as she went through the motions of having a procedure such as the D&C. As soon as she was healed, she went back to wanting to try and conceive again. Following her miscarriage, her fertility doctor tested her ovarian reserve and that's how she learned that she was pre-menopausal and her egg count was very low. She knew that time and age were a significant factor here and she wasn't ready to give up hope although it was dwindling.

After two more years of trying to conceive, failed IVF cycles, and a failed adoption, she and her partner decided that they were done trying to build their family further than the two of them. This decision was difficult and they didn't make it lightly. The possibility of not having living children had come up before in couples therapy as they tried to prepare themselves for future outcomes. They had decided that if it didn't happen, they would live a meaningful life but, first, they would give space to grieve their fertility journey.

Grief occurs from a death but also at the loss of something that impacts our life or worldview. Triggers don't vanish just because you've made a decision but knowing what your future will look like helps you cope to a fuller extent.

There can also be someone who has one or two living children and they want to have more, which is why they are trying to conceive in the first place. People who previously had a pregnancy (or multiple pregnancies) that led to living children can still experience infertility and pregnancy loss. Their grief may differ from someone who doesn't have living children but that's natural to anyone who has a differing experience. Grieving the size of your family not being what you had hoped for is devastating and when someone experiences pregnancy loss (or recurrent losses) then there is the possibility that their fertility journey could end in a loss and that's adding fuel to the fire that is grief.

How are you supposed to move forward when your path forward is blurred or uncertain? It's a fair question and the truth is, you just *do*. You survive, you keep moving through the days, you honor your emotions, lean on coping tools that you find helpful, and remember that you can grieve while also trying to enjoy the life you are living.

Some Things to Know After Pregnancy Loss (from a Miscarriage Doula)

Over the years as a miscarriage doula, I've identified some basic truths that I share with my clients:

- ◆ It's only in the most severe cases that a woman is responsible or to *blame* for her pregnancy loss. Even when something is seen as *preventable*, it's only preventable if you know that it exists and how to treat or prevent it.
- ◆ Hindsight basis happens for so many people after a death, and it can destroy the trust that you may have built in your body through pregnancy (or your first pregnancy, if that applies to you). You don't know what you don't know and without knowing something, you cannot prevent it from happening nor can you give yourself a warning.

- While pregnancy loss is common with roughly 25% of pregnancies ending in miscarriage or pregnancy loss, it's still taboo and stigmatized. Don't let the caveat of something being common erase the despair and grief that you feel.

- If anyone ever says miscarriage is normal, don't believe them. It's a *common* experience, not a *normal* one. It's an abnormal outcome for pregnancy, meaning that you're less likely to have pregnancy loss than have a living child from that pregnancy. It's not normal—it happens often, yes.

- During your fertility journey when you're trying to conceive, whether it's prior to a pregnancy or following pregnancy loss, if you feel uncomfortable with trying to conceive without medical guidance or have any concerns whatsoever about your health, it's okay—and valid—to seek the support of an OB/GYN or a fertility specialist.

- One of the reasons why loss happens is due to a chromosomal abnormality and sometimes people will do pathology testing (especially if they have a D&C or likewise procedure) and feel confused when the results come back *normal*. The testing that is done is not one that covers every genetic abnormality and it doesn't mean that it's your body or something within your control. There are so many reasons why death happens in utero and we have access to testing for a handful of them.

- The physical and emotional recovery from pregnancy will look different for everyone. Try (really hard) not to compare yourself to how others in your life have grieved pregnancy loss or how people on the internet seem to be handling theirs. The saying that grief *is not linear* is true—it's not the same for everyone and rarely do we have two people with 100 % matches for their emotional well-being and physical experience. You are a unique human being, and your life experiences will also be those things.

- Grief is grief and you are grieving.

Reflection Prompts

◆ Have you shared your loss/losses with anyone? If so, who knows and how did you share your story with them? Are they supportive?

◆ Is there someone in your life who you wouldn't share your emotions or experiences with due to how you anticipate their reaction? If so, who, and how do you anticipate that conversation going?

◆ What's one thing you've done to acknowledge your miscarriage, pregnancy loss, or baby?

To Move Forward, You Have to Keep Going

There are many difficult and hard things about pregnancy loss and grief in general but the fact that we must keep going to some degree is the hardest to grasp. What do you mean we have to keep caring for ourselves, working, maintaining friendships, all while going through one of the hardest times in our lives? It feels impossible at times (which is a valid way to feel). It's important to acknowledge that you aren't going to wake up one morning and find that everything is okay and the grief has disappeared. That's why I say "moving forward" and not moving on.

Through processing your pregnancy loss experience and tackling triggers along with the many topics that come up, especially in the first year after pregnancy loss, is exactly what moving forward looks like. It's not easy, it's not fun, but it's survival after grief.

People often ask me how they should respond to people who ask, "How are you?" following a miscarriage or loss, especially when saying "good" doesn't feel authentic. I often say "surviving" or "getting through each day the best I can" because that feels the most like getting through pregnancy loss.

Reflection Prompts

- What aspect of your life has changed the most since/because of this loss?
- In a perfect world, what would the next three months look like?
- Thinking about future pregnancies, what would make you feel more comfortable in your next pregnancy?

Epilogue

There's no easy way to move through life after experiencing the grief and trauma of any reproductive health issue such as infertility or pregnancy loss. It's a life-changing event that happens in what feels like the blink of an eye. We don't get to say goodbye to our naive self or make a disaster plan before the initial disaster. Everything shifts and changes without our consent and it's a lot to handle. That's why I became a bereavement doula, because I wanted to make a difference and help others navigate life after loss through teaching, sharing, and validating their experiences. It's exactly what I craved and what I couldn't find after each of my miscarriages. I read book after book and while memoirs were helpful in feeling emotionally less alone—a guidebook to each topic that would bring me grief would have been a gamechanger.

In 2018, when I had my first miscarriage, I went to social media for support and found many women who spread the messages of *never giving up* or *staying positive for a positive outcome* and I didn't relate to those outlooks. I thought that if I just complied with the belief of inviting positivity, I would never experience another miscarriage. Then my second miscarriage happened, and it felt like a cord snapped in half and was forever severed. I no longer believed those narratives because it felt like I was proof that they didn't work. That's when I became a loud voice on social media that others coined as *authentic* and *transparent* when in reality, I just wanted to be the voice I desperately needed to hear. In the end, it led me here, to The Miscarriage Doula, and writing this book that I hope will help others who relate to my approach and tone.

The biggest lesson that I learned from pregnancy loss and that I continue to highlight for others is that grief is subjective. It doesn't follow any rules or guidelines and what works for one person may not be helpful to another.

In my opinion, this is why we often feel isolated and alone, even if we have people around us. As I've approached in this book, there are many ways to experience pregnancy loss and grief has many shapes and sizes. It helps to find resources and people who have experienced an inkling of what you have to feel supported. There aren't many other types of death or loss in life that feel this difficult to navigate, especially on a societal level. After pregnancy loss, we are battling with grief, trauma, and societal expectations of how we should feel. It's a nightmare in many ways.

If you're holding this book while in the thick of your grief, please know you are not alone. Whatever you're feeling—anger, numbness, hope, fear—it's valid. There is no right way to move forward, only the way that feels right for you. Don't let anyone else dictate your grief. My hope is that we continue to build spaces where grief isn't hidden, and where reproductive trauma is acknowledged as the life-altering experience it truly is. That we shift from a toxic form of positivity to compassion and realistic storytelling. The fact that you picked up this book, read it, and made it to this page shows strength and hope for the future, so take a moment to feel pride in your grieving process. Grieving means being uncomfortable, which is not often a message we hear. I used to think that grieving should only feel like progress, but sometimes even progress doesn't feel right.

Take your time. Grieve as the days pass and keep moving forward.

Notes

Chapter 2: Understanding Pregnancy Loss

1. Bowlby, J. (1969). *Attachment and Loss*. Harmondsworth, Middlesex, England: Penguin Books. New York, NY: Viking Penguin.

2. Dewald, P.O. and Hoffman, J.T. (2025 Jan). Gestational Sac Evaluation. [Updated 2023 Jul 24]. In: *StatPearls [Internet]*. Treasure Island, FL: StatPearls Publishing. Available from: https://www.ncbi.nlm.nih.gov/books/NBK551624/.

3. Donovan, M.F., Arbor, T.C., and Bordoni, B. (2025 Jan). Embryology, Yolk Sac. [Updated 2023 Mar 6]. In: *StatPearls [Internet]*. Treasure Island, FL: StatPearls Publishing. Available from: https://www.ncbi.nlm.nih.gov/books/NBK555965/.

4. https://www.asrm.org/practice-guidance/practice-committee-documents/evaluation-and-treatment-of-recurrent-pregnancy-loss-a-committee-opinion-2012/.

5. Willinger, M., Ko, C.W., and Reddy, U.M. (2009 Sep 17). Racial disparities in stillbirth risk across gestation in the United States. *American Journal of Obstetrics and Gynecology* 201 (5): 469.e1–469.e8. https://doi.org/10.1016/j.ajog.2009.06.057.

6. Zamani, Z. and Parekh, U. (2020). "Vanishing Twin Syndrome," https://www.ncbi.nlm.nih.gov/books/NBK563220/.

7. Raymond, E.G., Harrison, M.S., and Weaver, M.A. (2019 Jan). Efficacy of misoprostol alone for first-trimester medical abortion: a systematic review. *Obstetrics and Gynecology* 133 (1): 137–147. https://doi.org/10.1097/AOG.0000000000003017. PMID: 30531568; PMCID: PMC6309472.

Chapter 3: The Many Layers of Grief

1. Kübler-Ross, E. (1970). *On Death and Dying*. New York: Macmillan. Available at: https://www.amazon.com/Death-Dying-Doctors-Nurses-Families/dp/1476775540.

2. Clewell, T. (2004). Mourning beyond melancholia: Freud's psychoanalysis of loss. *Journal of the American Psychoanalytic Association* 52 (1): 43–67. https://doi.org/10.1177/00030651040520010601.

3. "Grief Work: The Grief Theory of Erich Lindemann," https://whatsyourgrief.com/grief-work-grief-theory-erich-lindemann/.

4. https://whatsyourgrief.com/bowlby-four-stages-of-grief/.

5. https://whatsyourgrief.com/randos-six-r-processes-of-mourning/.

6. https://pmc.ncbi.nlm.nih.gov/articles/PMC7778565/.

Chapter 4: Trauma and Pregnancy Loss

1. Barlé, N., Wortman, C.B., and Latack, J.A. (2017). Traumatic bereavement: basic research and clinical implications. *Journal of Psychotherapy Integration* 27 (2): 127–139. https://www.stonybrook.edu/commcms/psychology/_pdfs/social_health/_camille_wortman/Barle%20Wortman%20and%20Latack%202017%20article.pdf.

2. Farren, J., Jalmbrant, M., Falconieri, N. et al. (2022 Mar 1). Prognostic factors for post-traumatic stress, anxiety and depression in women after early pregnancy loss: a multi-centre prospective cohort study. *BMJ Open* 12 (3): e054490. https://doi.org/10.1136/bmjopen-2021-054490.

3. Farren, J., Jalmbrant, M., Ameye, L. et al. (2016). Post-traumatic stress, anxiety and depression following miscarriage or ectopic pregnancy: a prospective cohort study. *BMJ Open* 6 (11): e011864. https://doi.org/10.1136/bmjopen-2016-011864.

Chapter 7: Your Relationships After Pregnancy Loss

1. Gold, K.J., Sen, A., and Hayward, R.A. (2010). Marriage and cohabitation outcomes after pregnancy loss. *Pediatrics* 125 (5): e1202–e1207. https://doi.org/10.1542/peds.2009-3081. Epub 2010 Apr 5. PMID: 20368319; PMCID: PMC2883880.

2. Ibid.

Chapter 8: Dealing with Recurrent Pregnancy Loss

1. Mumford, S.L., Garbose, R.A., Kim, K. et al. (2018). Association of preconception serum 25-hydroxyvitamin D concentrations with live-birth and pregnancy loss: a prospective cohort study. *The Lancet. Diabetes & Endocrinology* 6 (9): 725–732. https://doi.org/10.1016/S2213-8587(18)30153-0. Epub 2018 May 31. PMID: 29859909; PMCID: PMC6109429.

Chapter 10: Moving Forward (Not Moving On)

1. Yang, S.A., An, S.H., Kim, C.H., and Kim, M.S. (2023). An analysis of John Bowlby's mourning stages in family art therapy as a way to help the family mourning process. *Journal of Hospice and Palliative Care* 26 (2): 27–41. https://doi.org/10.14475/jhpc.2.23.26.2.27. PMID: 37753509; PMCID: PMC10519726.

Acknowledgments

Writing this book was a labor of love, and I am so appreciative of the support I've received along the way. First and foremost, I would like to thank my clients, for they have trusted me with the details of the worst days of their lives. Thank you for your time, energy, and for sharing your babies with me. Thank you to Ashante Thomas who reached out to me about writing this book and believed in it from the very beginning. A special thank you to my two-person book club, Laura, who shared in the excitement of getting to write my own book. Thank you to my close friend and an important piece of *The Miscarriage Doula*, Sarah Cocke, who truly lifts me up and believes in me every step of the way. And thank you to Kerry for all four of our babies (the two who aren't with us and the two who are) for they wouldn't exist without him. I hope that wherever our first two babies are, they are proud of us.

About the Author

Arden Cartrette is a doula, a writer, and a mom based in North Carolina. She is a Certified Birth and Bereavement Doula as well as a Certified Trauma Support Specialist. Born in New York to a Jewish family, she found the world fascinating from a young age. It was known that she was creating stories everywhere she went and there was never an age where those stories didn't bleed through her personality. Writing was a way that she was able to cope with the hardships of life and it was always a dream to write a book.

Since writing through hardship came naturally, she started an anonymous blog in 2017 to chronical the reality of navigating infertility in her 20s (which everyone told her wouldn't happen to a 26-year-old woman). The blog, titled *Hello Warrior* became bigger than she ever dreamed. It was a space where she shared about fertility testing and later, the two pregnancies that would end in missed miscarriages. The anonymity of the blog was removed following her first miscarriage because she felt frustrated from the shame and guilt and needed a way to say, "Here I am world, I had a miscarriage." And that was the space that later turned her writing project into a deeper passion to understand reproductive health but to also support others who were navigating pregnancy loss themselves.

With a love for science and medicine, on top of writing, she always dreamed of being a pharmacist but found it difficult to support herself through college. Then she ventured out into real estate, which led to marketing, and all of which helped her grow her blog. In 2020, she welcomed her first of two living sons and decided that she was ready to support others on a bigger platform and created *The Miscarriage Doula,* which during the uncertainty of COVID-19, was a virtual offering for women—and their partners—all over the world.

Arden continues to write (although most of it never sees the light of day) and enjoys spending time with her young children, who once felt like a far-off dream.

Index